Anam Cara
wisdom

Anam Cara
Wisdom

SPIRITUAL GUIDANCE
FROM YOUR PERSONAL CELTIC ANGEL

Donald McKinney

Ulysses Press

Published in the U.S. by Ulysses Press
P.O. Box 3440
Berkeley, CA 94703

First published as *Celtic Angels* in Great Britain
in 2005 by Hodder and Stoughton

ISBN10: 1-56975-549-3
ISBN13: 978-1-56975-549-5

Printed in the U.S.A.

Proofreader: Kat Brooks
Production: Lisa Kester, Matt Orendorff
Cover design: Lourdes Robles

Distributed by Publishers Group West

To my Mum and Dad, with all my love

Table of Contents

Acknowledgments

While researching this book, I traveled to many of the furthest corners of the United Kingdom and Ireland. To do so is to understand how special and magical this land is. On my journeys I met so many amazing people that it would be impossible to list all of you. But from the family that found me wandering lost in the back lanes of Pembrokeshire to the collector of apples on the top of Croagh Patrick, I thank you all for your time, your stories and your encouragement.

I would like to thank Diana Cooper in particular. Having worked together over the years, she has inspired me with her writing and trust in the angels. I would particularly like to thank her for her generous endorsement of this book. It means a lot to me.

When I started the Celtic Circle, I did so almost on a whim. Now, within two years, it has become one of the largest global Celtic networks. Who would have believed it? To all of you who have joined, came to my talks and workshops or contacted me by e-mail or letter, my most humble thanks. Knowing that you are there makes all the difference to me.

At Body & Soul, I would like to thank Roslyn, Kerry and David in the shop and Lynne, Dorothy, Ruth, Tracy and Agnes in the office for your continued interest and support. I apologize for the sudden flurries of demands that you all coped with like true troopers. I would also like to thank my agent Luigi Bonomi for his trust and reassurances and Rowena Webb, Jacqui Lewis, Naomi Watson and all the great team at Hodder Mobius for all the hard work and enthusiasm. Equally I would like to thank Ray, Claire, Beth and all the team at Ulysses Press for their hard work on producing this edition. I am so grateful for all the effort that has made *Anam Cara Wisdom* so special.

Finally I have to once again thank Donald Busby for, well, everything.

I have dedicated this book to my parents. As I was writing the first part of *Anam Cara Wisdom* in early 2004, they were both an inspiration to me. What can I say? Let's all of us make sure that every day *is* a "Good Day"!

Preface

Just above the alder trees, the full moon emerges from behind the black winter rain clouds that have shrouded it all night. Like pulling back heavy velvet curtains, the landscape around me is suddenly revealed in tones of silver, white and black. At my feet the creek chuckles away to itself as the waters tumble past. A rush of exhilaration flows through me as the moonlight catches the tips of the ripples and turns them into sparkles.

Then there is a sensation of not being alone. A feeling that someone has joined me. The hairs on the back of my neck prickle and I fight an urge to turn around. This site is sacred to me. I come here almost every day, and at the full moon I bring my crystals and wash them in the cold, clear, moon-kissed water. There is the spirit of this site, of course, and normally he sits facing me from the other side of the river on a boulder that no longer exists. Tonight, however, he is absent.

I use my inner sense, my intuition, to try to understand what is happening. It is as if another me, a ghost me, turns around and looks behind, while the real me stands still, facing out across the water towards the moon. I try to understand why I no longer feel on my own. And then I gasp, for standing there, in the meadow behind me, are hundreds of angels. Celtic Angels as far as the eye can see. All looking at me. All watching. And all waiting.

My heart leaps into my mouth as I contemplate the scene. Nothing is said, nothing happens. They are just waiting. I am unsure how to react. There is no guidance. No etiquette that I know of. No set of rules.

This was not the first time I had been aware of spirits. Many times as I walked the hills, meditated at sacred sites or visited magical places, I have sensed their presence. It was the first time, however, that I had actually seen them. So many of them. And it was the first time that I had felt the urgency of their presence. It was clear to me that night that the time had come for me to open up and acknowledge the Celtic Angels.

This was a big step for me. I have never felt drawn to the traditional saccharine, sterile images of angels either as mystical messengers of a white God or as cute cheeky cherubs. For me such angels were too much part of a Christian establishment; too much part of a remote, rigid and hierarchical Church. Yet, as I quickly discovered, every major world religion has its angels. And so just as there are Buddhist angels, or devas, there are Celtic Angels as well. And these Celtic Angels *are* angels that I can relate to, understand and work with.

Initially these beings would have worked with the Druids and then with the Celtic saints after the arrival of Christianity. Celtic Angels acted as long-time companions to saints such as Iona's St. Columba. They were believed to be all around and with us all the time. They acted as an Anamcara, or "soul friend": a confidant, companion and counselor all rolled into one. This relationship then is very immediate, intimate and demanding. But to work with your Celtic Angels is also incredibly rewarding, for they are more than mere messengers: they are free agents with their own personalities, ideas and plans. Yet above all they want to help us. They want us to see the spiritual world that surrounds us, to realize our role in it and ultimately to fulfill our Purpose of Life.

Celtic Angels were a part of everyday life for the Celt and would be consulted before any major decision was made, their blessing sought before any action was completed. Whether working or playing, traveling or at home, Celtic Angels were always there, waiting to help and guide. In many ways this can be summed up by the traditional greeting in Irish Gaelic that translates as, "Me and my angel wish you and your angel a good day."

This book, then, is a guidebook for all people on a spiritual journey to help them to form a relationship with their own Celtic Angels and understand why we are alive. It is based on my own personal experiences, those of people I have met, the Irish sagas and the lives of the Celtic saints.

In the first part, "Celtic Angels," we briefly examine the history of angels in many different religious traditions around the world before concentrating on the Christian portrayal. Exploring the unique nature of Celtic Angels, you will discover their spiritual world as well as their relationship with the Druids and the Celtic Christian saints.

In the next part, "Your Anamcara," you will discover how to work with your personal Celtic Angels. As we turn our eyes away from the material world and open up to spiritual influences, the Celtic Angels are there to help us. You will explore techniques such as dream work, visualization and meditation to become more open to the angelic presence. Practices are described that will allow you first a greater awareness of our angels and then, step by step, a deepening and strengthening of that relationship until you actually meet and learn how to work with your own Anamcara. Through them you will learn how to open up to other groups of spirits that are there to help you. In particular you will meet and work with your ancestors and soul families. These are two groups that the Celts felt particularly close to.

You need to do much more than simply learn to communicate with Celtic Angels. You have to use their knowledge and inspiring presence to enhance your own life. In the third part you will learn how to work with both your own Celtic Angels and other Celtic Angels to enhance and expand your spiritual awareness. We do this by examining the link between Celtic Angels and sacred sites, creativity and then our own emotional needs. The penultimate chapter takes this theme and expands it to everyday life. Through practical examples, it shows you how to take the angels to work, home and play. Drawing together all the teachings in this book, the final chapter helps you to begin to discover your own Purpose of Life by working through a series of exercises with your own personal Celtic Angels.

Since that night of the full moon, my life has changed completely. Celtic Angels are already waiting to help you too. Probably you sense them around you from time to time: the unbidden thought; the sudden insight; the strange urges or half-understood feeling while out in nature. These are all signs that the Celtic Angels are with you.

Working with the Celtic Angels is a glorious life-enhancing experience. I am almost jealous of you starting along this road for the first time. You are going to have so much fun, meet some incredible people, be encouraged to seek out sacred sites and grow to understand what your life is all about and how important and worthwhile it is not just to you but to all of us.

More importantly, you are going to learn to live with your Anamcara: an angel who is with you all the time, always on your side and always wants you to succeed. You will never be alone again. You and your Anamcara will make a formidable team. Together you will grow and expand as your own spiritual awareness and understanding develop. Together you will contemplate and seek to achieve your Purpose of Life. And together you will both win through!

Rejoice! My Anamcara and I welcome you and your Anamcara to the wonderful, exciting and loving world of the Celtic Angels.

A Note on Word Usage

Throughout the text the term *Anam Cara* as two words is used to signify the general concept of "soul friends," while *Anamcara* as one word refers to a specific "soul friend."

Anamcara is sometimes spelled *Anamchara*; in this text, the spelling *Anamcara* is used to facilitate the proper pronunciation of "ahn-im-KAR-uh."

PART ONE

Celtic Angels

ONE

A Brief History of Angels

The mountain of Sri Pada soars 7,360 feet up from the Sri Lankan central highlands. Viewed from the southwest it looks as if a huge pudgy finger is pointing skyward. The Tamils call it Svargarohanam, the Ascent to Heaven. However, it is neither its remarkable shape nor its size that has made this mountain sacred. It is that on the summit there is a boulder with an indentation that looks like a human footprint. For Buddhists this is the footprint of the Buddha, for Christians and Muslims it is the footprint of Adam. Hence the mountain's title in English: Adam's Peak.

According to legend, when Adam was expelled from Paradise this was the first spot on earth that his foot touched. Some stories say that he had to stand there on one foot for a thousand years before God relented and allowed him to descend to the fertile plains below. According to Valentinus' *Pistis Sophia*, written in the second century A.D., Jesus is reported to have appointed the angel Kalapataras as guardian over the footprint. Later Islamic traditions have it that Adam, stranded on the mountain top, so irritated the local angels that they eventually appealed to Allah and had him removed.

There is a tantalizing parallel here with the story of St. Patrick. When he was expelled from the British Church in the fifth century A.D., St. Patrick removed himself to Croagh Patrick (as the mountain is now called) in County Mayo in western Ireland. There he fasted for forty days as he tried to decide what to do. He so annoyed the local angels that eventually they granted him his wishes in order to get rid of him. Hence all the snakes were removed from Ireland and it will become covered in water seven days before the end of the world.

Angels, then, are active all over the planet. In this chapter we shall look at how they manifest themselves in different religious traditions and look for any common characteristics. We do need to remember, however, that each religion reflects its own cultural, historical and social background. So each people's experience, understanding and ability to describe angels will differ. Thus jungle dwellers could believe that angels live in trees, while desert people will revere spirits that are borne on the wind.

The word "angel" comes to us from the Greek *angelos*, meaning "messenger." It is easy to conjure up an image of Hermes, the winged message-taker. However, when we look further afield it is more difficult to find the word "angel" in other languages. This doesn't mean angels do not exist, only that they are perhaps seen in a different role or revealing different attributes. The Thai word *nang-faa* literally means "sky-woman." It is translated into English as "angel." The word carries with it ideas of beauty and feminine qualities of acceptance and understanding. But in the Buddhist religious texts it refers to the wisdom of the Buddha-Dharma. One word then has many different levels of meaning and can even be seen as the aspiration of Buddhists.

The exercises in this chapter are designed to help you to begin your spiritual work, and are meant to be fun as well as informative. They will encourage you to think about your own angels and how they might look and act, and the worlds that they inhabit.

Before you start you should find or buy a book with blank pages. This will be your Angel Journal. As you work through *Anam Cara Wisdom* you should write down in your journal all that happens to you; your thoughts and ideas; your dreams and anything else that you think might be relevant or significant.

The intention here is to help you to open up to the subtle world of the angels. As you begin to recognize them and their influences, your life will expand and become more rewarding and magical. Your Angel Journal is a celebration of this. When you reread it you will be able to share once again the excitement, amazement and love that your journey will generate. Let's start now.

OPENING UP YOUR ANGEL JOURNAL

Light a candle. As you do this, say, "As I light this candle, I call the angels to me." As an invocation, this simple ceremony is a beautiful way to start any angel work you do. Its sheer simplicity reminds us that there is nothing difficult in working with angels.

Take your journal and head the first page: My Angel. Now draw a picture of how you imagine your angel looks. Don't worry if you think you're no good at drawing. If you really want to, you can paste in a picture from a magazine. Take some time to think about what your angel could look like. Listen to your inner thoughts. Is the angel male or female? Fair or dark? Tall or short? Young or old? Angels will always appear to us in a form that we find most appealing, so the decisions you make here will be noted by your angels.

And now every time you open your book, you'll be reminded of your angel. As you work through this book, your understanding will become refined and more advanced. But never forget this was your first unpolished idea. As such it will always be very precious.

Once you are finished, sit for a few minutes and enjoy the calm and sense of achievement. When you are ready blow out the candle and say, "Thank you for the light." If there is any thin trail of smoke, wave your hands through it and see if the smoke forms any patterns for you. This could be a final inspiring gift to you from your Celtic Angels.

Shinto and Angels

Shinto is an ancient Japanese religion. Estimates vary but it is generally accepted that around 86 percent of the Japanese population follow some combination of Shinto and Buddhism. Perhaps as many as 57 million Japanese practice Shinto as their main religion.

The origins of Shinto are lost in the mists of time. Certainly by the fifth century B.C. it was an identifiable religion, being a mixture of nature worship, reverence of ancestors, divination techniques, hero worship and shamanism. It is a description that would almost fit Celtic traditions at this time too. Shinto teaches that humans are fundamentally good and it is only evil spirits that corrupt, and so the purpose of most Shinto rituals is to seek protection from these spirits by purification, meditation, prayers and by making offerings to the kami.

The kami are the Shinto deities and many people see them as the equivalent of our angels. They are not the great gods of Mount Olympus; rather they are more like spirits representing qualities, material objects and even ideas necessary for life, such as the sun, rain, mountains and fertility. Humans become kami after they die and are revered by their families. Like the *nang-faa* mentioned above, kami often manifest the attributes that we as humans aspire to.

Like many Celtic gods and goddesses, kami are often associated with particular places. Amaterasu Omikami, for example, is the ancestress of the Imperial Family and her shrine is at Ise. Shinto teaches that nature is sacred and so to be in touch with nature is to be close to the gods. Even individual objects such as boulders, trees or rivers can be worshiped as sacred spirits. Seeming to grow out of the trees that surround it, the small but beautiful Futarasan Shrine at Nikko is dedicated to the kami of Nikko's three most sacred mountains. All this the Celt would understand. For them religion was something you practiced with nature, as you walked among the trees or sat watching the ocean ebb and flow.

Kami are also associated with particular clans, and even heroic individuals were often seen as being either kami or imbued with the spirit of the kami. All Japanese emperors, except the current one, have been believed to be divine. The Ovama Shrine at Kanazawa is a good example of reverence to a former local lord. Again, the Celt accorded mythic status to their heroes. Equally the honorific title of Saint was given to people, holy in their life, who continued to bestow blessings on their people even after their death.

Some kami also manifest the attributes that we commonly think of as belonging to angels. They act as guardians and as teachers, showing people how to recover and pursue their spiritual paths. These kami were not, however, some kind of separate caste and the connection between these angelic workers and other kami, ancestor spirits and other spiritual entities is fluid. This is also true with Celtic Angels. It is our modern world that likes to classify, pigeonhole and isolate different types. In reality everything and everyone is far more complex than simple categorization would imply.

ANGELS IN SACRED SPACES

Open with your invocation: light a candle and say, "As I light this candle, I call the angels to me."

Take a few moments to sit quietly watching the flame. Feel the angels gather. When you are ready, think of where you live and the countryside around you. If you live in the city, think of parks or any wilderness near you or of places that you enjoy visiting.

Angels, like the kami, are drawn to sacred sites where the energy of the land is strong. As you think of the land around you, does any one place leap out? Is there somewhere that now, when you think of it, feels special? Why not take some time to go and visit that site?

This is a simple but enjoyable way of affirming to yourself that you do want to do angel work. Your time is precious so it is glorious to use some of it to acknowledge the angels who surround you.

Take a small token with you when you go to visit your special place. This could be a pebble you gathered at the beach; a couple of cookies you baked; maybe just a piece of fruit. It is merely a token of intent on your part and respect as well. Leave the token at your special place and while you are there take some time to sit quietly and think about angels and your own spiritual path. Write down in your Angel Journal any thoughts you have, or anything curious that happens to you on your way there and back.

As you sit with your candle anticipating all this, remember to smile. To be happy and to make other people happy is one of the key purposes of angel work.

When you are ready, blow out the candle, saying, "Thank you for the light."

Buddhism and Angels

As with Shinto, the lack of conventional Western-style gods is also largely true of Buddhism. This is the fourth largest religion in the world and is based on the teachings of the Buddha, the "one who has awakened," who was born around 563 B.C. His teachings, the Tripitaka, together with commentaries and traditions, or Sutra "discourses," form the common basis of the different forms of Buddhism.

The main belief of Buddhism is that through rebirth a person can learn to release their attachments and desires.

Ultimately they can even give up the idea of self, and at this point they achieve enlightenment.

For the Celt this idea is not unfamiliar. They too believed that only through living many lives could we come to realize that material wealth and comfort afford very little spiritual satisfaction. Only by rejecting those tawdry baubles could we then see the nature of our own spiritual self and through that the path back to the Godhead.

There are many references in the Buddhist Sutras to angels. In the Introduction to the Jâtaka, when the mother of the future Buddha became pregnant, four angels with swords gathered around to protect her and her baby from harm. This is rather similar to when the mother of the future St. Columba was pregnant. Then angels came to her in Armagh in Northern Ireland while she slept, and draped a cloak of many colors over her for protection.

Many commentators suggest that the Buddhist equivalent of angels is devas. There are many kinds of devas, however, and various Buddhist traditions view them differently. Some believe that they are beings who have been reborn from humankind. But this is a form of trap, for they live in a delightful soporific paradise where they want for nothing but are unable to detach from the self and so are unable to achieve Nirvana—a state of liberation and freedom from suffering. These devas are more like trapped spirits than angels.

Some traditions, such as Tibetan Buddhists, see devas more as emanations of bodhisattvas, enlightened beings who have forsaken their own entry into Nirvana in order to help others to achieve enlightenment. One example of this is Kwan Yin, Chenrezig in Tibetan. Kwan Yin is sometimes called the goddess of compassion and she feels the suffering of all sentient beings.

Another form of devas are the pre-Buddhist deities that have been inherited from local cultures. In these facets they show many similarities with the Shinto kami.

BEING A DEVA

In this exercise we will spend some time imagining what it would be like to be a deva trapped in the bliss of Paradise. While there is a serious intent to this exercise, it is also a lot of fun, even if it is rather indulgent and naughty!

First we need to plan. Light a candle and say your invocation. Take some time to sit quietly watching the candle and simply enjoying the sense of being there with the angels gathering around.

Now take your Angel Journal and write in it all the things you really like doing. Be totally honest with yourself. You and your angels will know if you try to fib. Your list may well include things such as eating chocolate cake, sunbathing, cuddling on the sofa with your partner or pet, a good bottle of wine, walking along the beach, reminiscing with old friends.

The plan is to be a deva for the day. Or at least an evening. Look at your list and plan a totally indulgent, over-the-top excess of pleasure and extravagance. As you bake the cake or buy the chocolates, you can tell everyone it's angel work!

And it is angel work, in a way. As you partake of your indulgences, enjoy every moment. Savor them. Value each one. But also recognize that you couldn't do this all day, every day. Try to imagine what that would be like. These treats and pleasures would become stale and no longer special. It's like when we go on vacation, I love sunshine and heat, yet after a few weeks of that I find I miss the more moderate and changeable weather that I am used to in Scotland. I begin to be grateful for the ordinary all the more.

Most people do not appreciate this. They spend their lives seeking more and more pleasure, unaware that, like the devas, these demands are not going to lead to ultimate salvation. When the devas do realize this, they begin the road to true enlightenment.

In one story the Buddha shows a group of followers a sow rooting about in the trash on the side of the road. In a past life, He explained, this was the highest of all the devas. But how can this be? the followers asked. Who would give up such wealth and luxury to become a pig? But of course that is the wrong question. A better question, the one that should have been asked, would be, How could anyone believe that such a luxuriant life as that led by the devas would lead to the ultimate spiritual goal? And so is revealed, by that short parable, not only the blinkered attitude of humankind, but also the silken trap.

When you have finished your planning, blow out the candle and say, "Thank you for the light." It is now time to enjoy, indulge and understand.

Hinduism and Angels

Hinduism is generally regarded as the oldest major organized religion in the world today, with the Vedas, among the most sacred of the Hindu texts, being composed around 1500 B.C. It has some 762 million followers, 13 percent of the world's population.

For the outsider, Hinduism is a confusing mixture of gods, goddesses, devas, spirits and other spiritual entities. These are all, however, merely facets or manifestations of the one supreme being: Brahma.

While there are no specific angels that can be easily identified, there are many spirits who fulfill the traditional angelic roles: protecting and guiding humankind, and inspiring spiritual development. Apsarases are angelic beings who specialize in giving sensual pleasure to the gods. Sometimes they descend to earth to beguile men with their beauty and skills, and so prevent evil deeds from occurring. Gandharvas are often portrayed as winged men. They are divine musicians who would please not only men, but the gods with their skill and knowledge.

This confusion of roles, types and hierarchies is common with Celtic traditions. Within the pre-Christian practices, Celtic Angels would have been only one of several spiritual families that Druids could have chosen to work with. The Celtic saints, however, would have been far less likely to work with the gods and goddesses that the Druids had favored and so it is only after the arrival of Christianity that angels became the pre-eminent spiritual beings that humans chose to work with. For although the Celtic Angels are with us all the time, it is only when we acknowledge them that their true work can begin.

BEING A GANDHARVA

Doing angel work is not only for us. Like gandharvas, we can use our angel work and skills to help others.

Light a candle and say your invocation. Now sit quietly and watch the flame. Take some time to think of ways in which you can help others to open up to the influence of their angels. You might spend some time writing a poem or short story for them. This might inspire them to think about angel matters. Like the gandharvas, you might play some music for them. Or you might simply take your family on a picnic to a sacred site. Whatever you decide, make it fun and enjoyable.

Write down your intentions in your Angel Journal. And plan to do it within the next week. When you are ready, blow out the candle and say your words of closure.

Once the event is over come back and think about your expectations and how it went. Did you feel the angels working with you to make it a success? What lessons did you learn?

Islam and Angels

It was the Archangel Jibrael (Gabriel) who read the first revelation to Muhammad in Mecca in A.D. 610. After Abraham,

David, Moses and Jesus, Muhammad became convinced that he was the last of the prophets, his role being to clarify and purify the faith. Although the youngest of the major global religions, Islam is nonetheless the fastest growing and it is expected that by the mid-twenty-first century it will be the largest religion in the world. Today it has about 1.2 billion followers.

Islamic angels do not take human form. They may, however, appear in various guises in dreams and visions. Everyone has two Guardian Angels who watch, record and (implicitly) judge all that people do. Other angels attend mosques where they record the prayers of the faithful. There are four archangels: Jibrael, Mika'il, Israfil, who will sound the trumpet on the last day, and Izra'il, who is the angel of death. A jinn (genie) often appears in Arabic folk tales as a helper and guardian but in Islam they are seen as demons.

The rigidity and monotheism of Islam would, however, be difficult for the Celts to accept. Nonetheless, while the concept that an angel would judge you is alien to Celtic thinking, the idea of a Guardian Angel who is constantly with you is one that they would be able to appreciate.

ANGELS AS SPIRITS

Light a candle and say your invocation. Sit still for a few minutes watching the flame.

Angels are spirits. They have no body. Try to imagine what that would be like. You would be unable to touch anything; you would have no taste or sense of smell. No clothes or make-up. No sensual connection to the world at all.

Now take your Angel Journal and try to write a short monologue. Imagine you are a spirit, explaining to a new arrival what it's like to be in your world.

When you are ready, blow out your candle and say your words of closure.

The aim of this exercise is to make us appreciate that the world of the angel is so unlike anything we know here on earth that it is almost impossible for us to understand what it is like to be a spirit.

Judaism and Angels

Like Islam, Judaism accepts the teachings of the Prophet Abraham. Founded around 2000 B.C., Judaism is constructed on the covenant then entered into by Abraham and his God. It is the religion that is the historical basis of both Christianity and later Islam and much of the angel lore that is common to all three religions stems from Judaic teaching, some of it up to 3,000 years old.

Unlike Christianity or Islam, however, there is no angel worship or belief in Guardian Angels and humans would only encounter angels where these beings are undertaking God's work. Rabbi Judan teaches in the Talmud that, if in trouble, people should not appeal to angels but only to God alone.

There are seven archangels, of which the best known are Gabriel, Michael, Raphael and Uriel. Angels act as messengers of God, based on the belief that humans are unable to bear to look on the countenance of God. They have no human form and even biblical descriptions are believed to be metaphorical rather than literal.

This monotheism of the Jews would feel uncomfortable to the Celt. They knew there were spirits all around them. They consulted and worshiped them continually. Celtic religions did not believe in one omnipotent omnipresent divine figure and so Celtic Angels were believed to be free spirits with their own personalities and agendas.

THE ANGEL IN THE BURNING BUSH

Light a candle and say your invocation. Sit still for a few minutes watching the flame. In this exercise we are going to try to consider different meanings from the story of the angel on Mount Sinai. The text in the Bible reads:

> Now Moses kept the flock of Jethro his father in law, the priest of Midian: and he led the flock to the backside of the desert, and came to the mountain of God, even to Horeb. And the angel of the Lord appeared unto him in a flame of fire out of the midst of a bush: and he looked, and, behold, the bush burned with fire, and the bush was not consumed. [Exodus iii, 1–2, King James Version]

In seeking to understand this popular story, first think about it for a few minutes and seek inspiration from the whispers of the angels all around you. To begin with, of course, there is the literal meaning: what does this passage describe?

Next consider the metaphorical meaning: what does it seem to suggest by using the words it does? Caution has to be added here because, as we have already noted, this is a translation. What, we might ask, was the intent of the authorities who approved this translation?

Finally, we need to consider the hidden meaning. This is the discovery of the true spiritual meaning of this passage.

Write down your answers. Return later and consider them again. You may well find that some of your ideas have changed.

Sit still and when you are ready blow out the candle and say your words of closure.

The point of this exercise is to warn against taking anything written down too literally. We have already seen the problems of translation with the concept of *nang-faa*. Any writing is an attempt to compress human experience into strokes of ink on paper and as such can never be totally precise.

The Celtic Druids recognized the danger of this and forbade any of their work to be written down. Even today we should respect that.

The problem is that we have lost the skill of memorizing large amounts of material. We need written information to prompt and remind us. Your own Angel Journal will mean far more to you than it will to anyone else who may read it. You will remember the incidents you describe, together with the subtleties of the emotions felt and actions of others. Only you will know why you chose to describe a sensation one way rather than another. And, even accepting all that, your Angel Journal will remain more of a prop for you to recall particular incidents, rather than a complete recording of the incident itself.

What all this shows is the danger of simply accepting at face value whatever is written. You need constantly to seek to understand any material you read, but, especially with spiritual work, it should resonate with you on some level. Your own personal experience is far more important than any book. What I hope a book like *Celtic Angels* will do is help to suggest ways for you to progress in your angel work and also put into some context events and sensations that you may already be experiencing. And, as in all work, if it doesn't feel right and comfortable, don't do it!

What Is an Angel?

Given the vastness of the global experience, it is almost impossible to draw up any generalized definition of what an angel is. There are, however, a few points that we can make. The first is that they are spirits. Some traditions have it that they can take corporeal form if it is necessary for their work. Other peoples believe that they remain invisible.

Angels do seem to be attracted to particular sites on earth. Many mountains are sacred, such as Mount Kailash in Western Tibet where Shiva and Parvati lie together in bliss. Where rivers merge is another powerful spot, such as Kataragama, the holiest place in Sri Lanka. There Muslims come to seek teachings from al-Khadir, the revealing angel referred to in the Qur'an. The site is also sacred for Buddhists, Christians and Hindus.

Angels seem to straddle the physical, spiritual divide. They are of the spiritual realms but seem able and willing to walk in this world too. Thus they can communicate the desires of the gods to humans but equally, in some traditions, represent human concerns and attitudes to the gods.

Angels also seem to seek to offer help to people. As well as revealing the spiritual world to us and often the word of the gods, they also frequently assist us in much more mundane ways, helping us to avoid danger and providing us with inspiration.

Many of the world's religions, such as Judaism, Christianity and Islam, are founded on angel teachings. In 1827 it was the angel Moroni who appeared at Palmyra, New York and led Joseph Smith to the golden tablets that make up the Book of Mormon and so to establish Mormonism as a religion in America.

In the next chapter we look at the role of angels in Christianity and will show that it is far more complex and intriguing than we might at first expect. We will then go on to explore the relationship between the Druids and angels and then the relationship between the Celtic saints and their heavenly companions. And we will discover that the Celtic Angels are very much angels for today!

TWO

Christian Angels

In the Western world, it is the Christian images of angels that dominate our lives. We are surrounded by pictures of angels as cute cherubs, on everything from greeting cards to toilet paper. Yet Christianity is an extremely diverse religion and attitudes toward angels vary widely as well. In this chapter we shall explore how Christians see angels and how the look of the angel has changed quite dramatically through time.

Types of Christianity

Most Christians believe that Jesus was the Son of God. Within a few years of his death, around A.D. 30, there were three clearly identifiable Christian sects. Within Judaism there were a group of followers of Jesus; St. Paul led a movement aimed primarily at converting non-Jews; and finally there were the Gnostic Christians who emerged from the Essene movement. The Jewish Christians were killed or scattered by the destruction of Jerusalem in A.D. 70. Pauline Christianity was legalized in A.D. 313 and became the official religion of the Roman Empire in A.D. 380. The Gnostics were either absorbed into the Church or exterminated as heretics.

Schisms continued, with the Oriental Orthodox and Assyrian Churches splitting in A.D. 451. The Eastern Orthodox Churches split from Rome in 1054 and the two sides excommunicated each other. In 1517 Martin Luther, a Christian monk, set out to reform the Catholic Church. This eventually led to the rise of Protestantism across much of northern Europe. In 1534 the Church of England rejected the interference, as they saw it, of the Pope. Today the Anglican (or Episcopalian) Communion stretches all over the world headed by the Archbishop of Canterbury, who is still appointed by the British Queen on the advice of her Prime Minister.

The Bible

The one thing that almost all Christian traditions have in common is that they derive their authority from the Bible. However, with almost 34,000 different Christian groups, there are many different views on not just what should be in or out of the text of the Bible, but even how we should approach the Bible itself.

Unlike almost every other book, different editions contain different material. Nearly all versions carry the same thirty-nine books of the Old Testament and twenty-seven books of the New Testament. However some gospels, such as the Book of Jasher, are referred to in the Bible (2 Samuel i, 18; Joshua x, 13) but are not in most versions today. Some Church Bibles include a set of Old Testament gospels called the Apocrypha, others do not. One of these gospels is the Book of Tobit, which recounts Tobias' journey with the Archangel Raphael, the only place where such an archangel is mentioned. Protestant Bibles normally do not include the Apocrypha but Catholic Bibles do. The Ethiopian Church includes the Book of Enoch in their scriptures; other Christian traditions warn against the very same gospel for here the angels are all too human, taking mortal wives who then bear them monstrous children called the Nephilim.

Putting aside what should or should not be in the Bible, even the approach taken to it varies from one Church to another. For some the Bible is the actual Word of God. They argue that the authors of the texts were inspired by God and since God cannot be in error, then their writings are also without error.

Others argue that the Bible contains the Word of God but also has passages that are clearly against the will of God, such as those condoning slavery, genocide or the torture of prisoners, and so these passages must be rejected. An example of one of these passages is Exodus xxi, 20–21, which argues that it is all right to strike a servant with a rod, so long as you don't kill them. Or rather so long as they live for at least two more days. The existence of such passages means that there is considerable scope for interpreting what is and is not the will of God. One example of this would be the role that women should play in the community today.

Finally, it is possible to argue that the Bible is a wide-ranging human document written by human and thus fallible people. They incorporated a lot of pagan material, such as the creation myths, and values and outlooks of people from more than 2,000 years ago. It is then a document to inspire and inform us but it is not one we should take as a literal guide of how to live our lives today.

Angels in the Bible

In the Bible, angels appear as messengers, guides and healers. They also make up the Celestial Court where they serve God and sing His praises. Unlike Jews, who see angels as emanations of God, Christians see angels as free-thinking, independent spirits created by Him when He created the material world. St. Augustine argued that angels were simply spirits and it was the nature of the office that allows us to call them angels, for "in as far as he exists, an angel is a spirit, and as far as he acts he is an angel."

Angels are mentioned at least 108 times in the Old Testament and 175 times in the New Testament. Clearly they play a major role and are often portrayed as God's messengers on earth. Generally they are believed to be sexless, though that is not explicitly stated in the Bible. When they appear in the Bible they are almost always adult males and rarely do they have wings.

Angels can appear in solid corporeal form. Hebrews xiii, 2, warns: "Do not forget to entertain strangers, for by so doing some people have entertained angels without knowing it." This implies that angels are able to eat and drink as well. Celtic saints would have recognized this, and there are many tales told of such encounters. In one, St. Cuthbert welcomes a stranger in from the winter cold and gives him his own food. In return the visitor leaves freshly baked bread still warm from some unknown celestial oven.

Being able to take solid human form, angels must be able to change things in the material world too. Angels opened the prison doors for the apostles in Acts v, 19. They can also affect the natural world, such as controlling the winds (Revelation vii, 1–3).

As free-thinkers, angels possess quite distinct personalities and exhibit personal preferences. Angels are also capable of emotions such as joy, desire and choice (Luke xv, 10; 1 Peter I, 12; Jude 6).

Of course you will never know if you have been touched by such an angel, for, despite the story above, it is rare that they reveal themselves. The same St. Cuthbert told a tale of his youth where, becoming lame, he was unable even to walk. Sitting in the sun one day he was approached by a stranger who advised him how to treat his lameness. This he did and was soon running around again. St. Cuthbert was convinced that this stranger was an angel. But who can tell?

In our own lives it is a challenge to treat all strangers as angels. The following exercise merely illustrates how difficult it is. That doesn't mean, however, that we shouldn't keep attempting to live up to our own expectations. And like St. Cuthbert you may never know if you have helped or been helped by an angel, but perhaps that is part of the fun of it all!

STRANGERS AS ANGELS

Every day, especially in towns and cities, we are constantly meeting and coming into contact with people we don't know. Most of them are no doubt other mere mortals just like us, but what if some were angels? And we ignored them, or were rude to them or spurned their pleadings for help? What would that say about us? And, let's be honest, what does it say about us if these beings were mere humans just like us?

When we meet strangers, there is always a point in that meeting. There is an exchange, we give something and receive something in return. If we are helpful to a tourist, we give them information and hopefully a friendly impression of where we live. In return, as well as the satisfaction of helping someone, we might hear a little of where the person is from, or how they are enjoying their trip or maybe even information on a tourist site that we, as locals, have neglected to visit.

If someone asks us for money, the exchange obviously is that we give them some cash, while in return they may make us feel a little bit better about ourselves, or at least appreciate the differences in our respective situations. If we take the time, we might learn a little about the problems of having no permanent place to stay. This should help us to appreciate how lucky we are.

Each day describe in your journal all such encounters that happen to you, or even ones that you deliberately avoided. Ask yourself if you behaved honorably. Would you be happy if the stranger had been an angel? One day, quite possibly, you may even sense somehow that the being was indeed divine.

Types of Angels

The Bible lists nine types (or choirs) of angels. The most senior are seraphim, the attendants on God, listed only once in the Old Testament. Such is their divine presence that they are rarely perceived by humans. They have three sets of wings: one set covers their face, another their feet and the third is for flying. Cherubim are the next most senior. Descriptions of them vary; Ezekiel x, 14, describes them as having four faces: cherub, human, lion and eagle. In Revelation iv, 8, they are "living beasts" with many eyes and six wings that constantly praise God. The name cherubim is derived from the Hebrew *kerub*, which means "fullness of knowledge." They hold the divine wisdom and educate the lower levels of angels. They also have a role as guards. God placed two of them with flaming swords at the gates of the Garden of Eden to prevent Adam and Eve from returning.

Thrones are characterized as angels of peace and submission. They exist where material form begins to take shape and are often portrayed as vast chariot wheels with many eyes. God rests on them. The lower choirs of angels need the thrones to access God.

Dominions are the angels who regulate the lower levels, and pass on the will of God. Virtues carry out the wishes of the dominions. They regulate the seasons and the natural world, though lower orders of angels have direct responsibility for such tasks. Powers are the warrior angels who fight against evil throughout the universe. Curiously, they are led by angels of darkness.

Principalities are angels who watch over human cities and nations, the visible aspects of human life. Archangels are beings who can belong to other categories too, such as St. Michael who is also listed as a seraphim. Archangels carry out the will of God, and are also in charge of the Guardian Angels.

Catholics recognize Gabriel and Raphael as archangels too, while other traditions list additional ones. The Bible itself is ambiguous on this issue.

Angels, rather confusingly a category on their own, are those closest to humans. They are couriers delivering prayers to God and His replies. They also mirror the will of God. It is the last two categories, archangels and angels, that we, as mere mortals, are most likely to come across.

Angels and Christianity

Most Christians, because of their common heritage and belief in the Bible, see angels in similar ways. Angels are intermediaries between humans and their God. They act as messengers and also attend God where they sing His praises. The important angels are the Archangels Michael, Gabriel and Raphael. Christians accept that angels play a major role in both Christian history and human life today. Catholics believe that it is rare, however, for a person to hear an angel. Catholic teaching stresses that angels, because they have no permanent corporeal form, tend to speak in a person's mind rather than from outside like other humans would.

Catholics also believe that each person has their own Guardian Angel whom they ask for help in human affairs. These angels can only try to influence others, however, and cannot force them to act in any specific way. Historically these angels played a small role in the Church until the seventeenth century when, following a rapid increase in interest, the Church responded with a special day of celebration on October 2nd each year.

Some Protestant Churches are uncomfortable with this, seeing it as coming very close to breaking the biblical instruction not to worship an angel (Revelation xxii, 8ff). They believe that angels are here to protect us and we should be aware of that but we should not pray for their help or guidance. Rather we should pray to God and His will may cause the angel to appear in our lives.

Then there is, of course, Lucifer, who was a seraphim but rebelled against God and was expelled with around a third of the angelic host. He now presides over Hell and seeks to lure people into sin. Some Gnostic sects believe this is too literal a translation of the Bible and suggest that the truth is that it is the material world that is "Hell" because when we are on earth we cannot be in Heaven. We are stuck here because of our physical desires: the seven deadly sins, and only when we reject them can we escape the earth plane and return to the heavenly realm. Gnostics do not see Lucifer as some demon; rather he is the guardian of the earth. It is through his creation that we are able to learn our lessons and so return to our rightful place.

Angels and Art

Since probably the beginning of time humans have sought to portray angels in their art. Angels, or angel-like creatures, can be found in work from Mesopotamia, Egypt, Greece and India, among others. Hindu, Buddhist, Zoroastrian, Jewish, Islamic and Christian artists have all sought to portray angels, often using the likeness as a doorway to another spiritual realm. Stained glass in church windows is one example where this could be literally true and where nature (in the form of sunshine) could come together with the artist to form something that was a spectacular celebration of the divine.

Angels as winged beings have appeared since ancient times too. Wings were seen possibly as a symbol for spiritual travel. Earliest images have been traced back to 6000 B.C. but it is in the portrayal of the goddess Isis in 1800 B.C. that we find the first clear depiction of a winged being. The image of

Isis and of other goddesses of the middle Egyptian Cultural period is very identifiable to us as an angel. The first male image is the Angel of Nimrud, found in a sculpture relief on the Assyrian palace walls and created around 875 B.C. Winged lions, horses, sphinxes and bulls abound in Middle East archaeology and here the presence of wings may well underline the divinity of these beings. Of course the presence of wings might also simply be a representation of humanity's desire to be able to fly like birds. The idea is that those beings who can fly must be more (spiritually) advanced than those same beings who cannot.

Around 500 B.C., the ancient Greeks adapted the Isis image to Nike, the victory aspect of Athena and created the archetypal angel likeness that we all recognize today. Byzantine art, which was to have such a profound influence on the Celtic scribes, derives many of its ideas from the Greeks, and by around A.D. 500 the popular image of the angel was sealed.

It may seem surprising that the Hebrews did not offer us any imagery, given that so much of our knowledge of angels comes from their writings, but Hebrew art was too iconoclastic and so precluded angelic images.

It was only at the Renaissance that we see the next major development in the portrayal of angels. This occurred with the introduction of the putti, or cherubs as we call them now. These cuddly, chubby baby boys are often seen dancing or making music. They are not, however, strictly speaking angels and although we call them cherubs, they should not be confused with the mighty cherubim. Ironically, in the West when people think of angels, the image of the cherub is the one that comes most easily to mind.

In Islamic art the archangels are often portrayed almost metaphorically. Mika'il (Michael) is covered in fine hairs of saffron and his wings are green topaz. On each hair he has a million faces and on each face a million eyes. Jibrael (Gabriel) has become, as in the Christian image, an androgynous delicate figure.

SEEKING IMAGES OF ANGELS

Take some time to find pictures or drawings of angels and add them to your Angel Journal. Try to understand why some images attract you more than others. It might be the colors, or that some are more overtly Christian than others. Or maybe it is the opposite. Or perhaps it is the way the angel or archangel is portrayed. Gradually, as you accumulate images, you will begin to see patterns in what pictures attract you more than others. Write down your thoughts in your Angel Journal.

New Age Angels

It is a paradox that at a time when interest in established Christian religion has never been lower (at least in the West), interest in angels continues to grow. People no longer relate to the Churches as they once did. But this is not to say that they are not concerned about matters spiritual. Many commentators argue that interest has never been higher. New age writers and teachers have, to some extent, filled this gap between established religion and people's needs.

Writers such as Diana Cooper, Doreen Virtue, William Bloom and Rosemary Ellen Guiley are among an ever increasing band of people who help others to understand and access the angel energies that are all around us. While in the main they use Christian imagery, and even language, to describe the angelic experiences, they nonetheless do so in a non-doctrinal, non-judgmental way. They do not isolate themselves or condemn other traditions. Hence many of these writers will use examples and belief systems that owe more to Hinduism, Buddhism or even paganism than to Christianity.

The early 1960s saw the foundation, by a group of committed Christians, of a community at Findhorn, in northeast Scotland. There cooperation between nature spirits, or nature-devas as they are sometimes called, and humans led to the creation of a highly fertile garden on what had previously been moor and wasteland. Still flourishing today, Findhorn is a living example of what humans and angels, working together, can achieve.

Findhorn also illustrates how our human words can influence how we view the spirit world. In the 1960s angels were seen by many "modern" Christians as being equated with outmoded concepts of a patriarchal, hierarchical Anglo-Saxon arch-conservative view of religion. Struggling to invent a new vocabulary to reflect the world more accurately as they saw it, they started referring to angels as sprites or nature spirits. To us today this suggests fairies rather than angels, but the distinction has at times been quite blurred. Hill of Angels on the Scottish island of Iona, for example, was traditionally called An Sithean in the Gaelic, or Fairy Hill. In all likelihood this was its name even in St. Columba's time. It seems that the name was changed, at least in English, with the revival of interest in St. Columba in the seventeenth century. Once again we find human language unable to describe adequately the magic world of angels.

WORKING WITH NATURE SPIRITS

Choose a couple of plants to work with in this exercise, which will actually be an ongoing experience for you. If you have a garden you might choose a small corner. If you live in an apartment, ask your friends for some plants or simply go out and buy a couple.

Nature spirits tend all plants and trees. To make it easy for yourself try, if you can, to choose bushy, thick plants. It is much easier to imagine little sprites and fairies hiding in the extensive foliage.

Create a little ceremony where you welcome, or acknowledge, the plants and the nature spirits. Offer them true unconditional love. One way of doing this is to sit facing the plant. Place one hand on each side of it. If it is not too delicate you might lay your hands on the leaves. Ask the plant for permission to love it. Almost certainly you will feel a positive response. If not, respect that and try again a few days later. When you are able to proceed, simply feel love radiating out from you, feel it reach from one hand to the other through the plant. Note down in your Angel Journal how love feels in this situation.

Leave small gifts. Tend the plants carefully. Praise them when new leaves or flowers appear. Above all, try to see the plants as not just material things but as having a spiritual dimension as well.

You might find this difficult at first, you may even feel a little silly. The truth is that the plants will respond. The nature spirits themselves might begin to talk to you and you need to listen to any thoughts that seem suddenly to appear in your mind from nowhere, especially if they involve the care of the plants.

The main value of this exercise is that it helps us to open up to the idea that there is more to all of us than simply the material world that we can appreciate with our five senses. Working with plants and being out in nature quickly reveals to us just how narrow and insubstantial so much of our ordinary perceptions of the world really are.

It was this awareness that was to play so important a part in the development of Druidism and later Celtic Christianity. And so Celtic Angels can only truly be understood and appreciated when we acknowledge the spirituality of the natural world that lies all around us. As we will see, while conventional Christianity began to trap religion in huge stone mausoleums, the Druids, and then the Celtic monks, worshiped in the open air, appreciating the inspiration, wonder and magic of our own landscapes.

THREE

Celtic Angels

Every major culture and religion recognizes some form of angelic beings and the Celts were no different. When Rhygyfarch tells us that the sixth-century St. David was warned in advance of his death by an angel, he did not report that the saint's fellow monks seemed surprised, either at the presence of an angel, or the being's ability to prophecies. Rather only that they were overcome with grief at the thought of the saint's imminent death.

The original Celtic tribes probably originated in north India. Legends there speak of great political and social upheavals around 1500 B.C. It is just possible that these events saw the beginning of the Celts' move westward. By 700 B.C. there were Celtic settlements in central Europe. By the sixth century B.C., Greek writers such as Hecateus of Miletus were referring to the Keltoi. The Celts probably arrived in northern Italy around this time and shortly thereafter in northern Spain. In the fifth century B.C. they appeared in France and soon afterward in Britain and Ireland.

In their journey they would have come into contact with Hinduism, Judaism, Zoroastrianism, Greek philosophy and the Roman pantheon of gods. We do know that the Celts, as they migrated, integrated existing religions into their own religious traditions. It is impossible that they were not aware of the different forms of angel lore. As pragmatic people they would have looked around them and used the best of other cultures to help to understand their own spiritual experiences. This chapter seeks to explore how angels fit into the Celtic religious tradition.

For the Celt there was not the division between spiritual and material worlds that we see today. To them, humans were almost unique beings in that we are able to walk in the material world yet appreciate the existence of and communicate with the spiritual. Angels then were not rarefied creatures who only appeared occasionally. Rather they were part of everyday life. They were not worshiped or revered; nor were they feared. Rather they were respected companions.

In addition, for the Celt there was no formalized hierarchical society. Leaders were selected on merit, not birth, and this equality is reflected in the realm of the Celtic Angels. There is no rigid hierarchy based on title or power such as we see in other traditions. Instead distinctions, were they do exist, seem to be based more on the knowledge and experience of the Celtic Angels rather than any strict caste.

Because of their belief in the magic of the land, it is not surprising that some sites are associated with Celtic Angels. But for the most part, the angels seem to have been attracted more to the person than the place. And in some cases, like the hauntingly dramatic Carningli in Pembrokeshire, southwest Wales, the two ideas are fused, with the Hill o' Angels named after St. Brynach, who used to retreat to its craggy peaks to commune with his angels.

The Celtic gods and goddesses were very localized. There is no great pantheon of beings worshiped throughout the Celtic lands. After Christianity arrived, this tradition continued with most people worshiping local saints rather than God, Jesus or the Virgin Mary. Indeed, in Scotland, there is no record of any church being dedicated to the Virgin Mary until well after the Romanization of the Church had been all but completed, some time after the eleventh century.

The Celts believed that death was merely a stopping point and held no fear of it. Indeed, it was a celebration because it meant that the soul was free from this life and able to proceed to the next stage. Possibly following on from their Hindu roots, the Celts believed that the soul was reborn again and again as it progressed. They had no concept of Heaven or Hell, but believed that our ultimate goal was to rejoin the Godhead. And to do that we had to learn to resist the lure of the material world.

I find all this easier to understand if I imagine that the Godhead is the sun, blazing across the heavens. Within each one of us there is a tiny golden divine spark. That spark was once part of the Godhead. Like our own sun, the flames flare out from the golden orb, and sometimes the millions of tiny sparks that make up the huge flames simply blaze out too far across space and get trapped in the gravity of earth, the material plane.

Once there the spark gets pulled deeper and deeper into the atmosphere until its focus turns from the sun above to the earth below. Such is the pull of the earth now that the spark even forgets its divine home. Only slowly over a great period of time does the spark begin to become aware that there is more to life than a simple material existence. Life after life it is reborn, slowly progressing from single-cell creatures up through plants and trees to mammals and eventually to human. Only now can it begin to think of the Godhead once again. Maybe, occasionally, it will even feel the slightest pull.

Eventually, the divine spark is able to leave the physical world behind and progress to the world of spirit. It still has a long journey until it has truly put the material urges behind it and is able once again to reach for the sun.

Perhaps, then, it is no coincidence that humans have always worshiped the sun. It may be that the sun is the nearest physical manifestation we have to the Godhead.

WORSHIPING THE SUN

What we really mean here is celebrating the existence of the sun. Clearly we know, as the ancient Celts did, that the sun is a star not a god. For the Celts it was nonetheless special and worthy of worship. After all, their whole way of life would have been destroyed if the sun had not risen each day.

Find images of the sun and on a particular day, perhaps the first of each month, take some time to sit and think about the golden globe. Think about when you last noticed it. Perhaps you were sunbathing. Or maybe you were driving the car and it was blinding you.

Now ponder on the idea of the soul flames seeking to return to the Godhead, yearning, longing to be reunited. Try to imagine what it would be like to feel that emotion. Understand how you would have to reject all the comforts, delights and excitements that the material world offers.

On the first of each month, wait and see how long it is before you see the sun. It may be there when you awake or, during the cold gray weeks of winter, you may have to wait several days before the brilliant watery sun emerges to cheer everyone up. When you do, bow to it and, in your own mind, give thanks for its continued existence.

This small exercise is very precious because it connects the spiritual and the natural world in a clear and inspiring way. Enjoy worshiping the sun!

The Angelic Realms

Within the Angelic Realms there are many different levels. Some spirits are so close to the earth that they get caught up in human affairs and find it difficult to break away. These are the spirits who are all around us. They attach themselves to everything that exists and seek pleasure from being in contact with the physical world.

These spirits are deprived of the sensual pleasures and emotional charges of being human and yet seem unable to break the chains of attraction. Like the Buddhist devas they are caught in a silken trap of comfort and bliss. Like us they need to learn the lessons to allow themselves to progress on to the next stage.

At the next level, the spirits are beginning to look towards the Godhead. These are spirits who are still attracted by the world of humans, but recognize that there is more to the universe than simply the material world. It is as if they can hear the song of the Godhead and, while they remain close to the earth, they are looking over their shoulders at unseen desires.

The third level is for those spirits who have remembered that the reason for their existence is to find their way back to the Godhead and who have broken free of the earth and are drifting towards the Godhead. Because of their knowledge and understanding, these are the most advanced beings. Equally, they are the ones we are least likely to come across, as human life no longer has any attraction for them.

Pre-Christian Gnostics tended to present everything in an absolute, concrete way, and they argued that when spirits felt ready they would approach the gateway to the next level and be asked a question by the gatekeeper. If they could not answer the question then they had to return and live another life. If they answered the question correctly then they could progress to the next level. The Celts may not have believed that literally, but it is clear that no one, human or spirit, could progress until they had learned the lessons they had been born to learn.

What Are Celtic Angels?

Following St. Augustine's teaching that it is what a spirit does that makes it into an angel, it is clear that there are three main roles that angels can play. First, they can interact with humans and so make us aware of the spiritual realms. Second, it is said that they act as messengers from God to humans and sometimes vice versa, and, finally, that they look out for us, acting as Guardian Angels.

Celtic Angels are spirits who take a special interest in the affairs of humans. They seek out people who are becoming more aware of the spiritual dimensions of their own life and try to help them to progress. Through them, people learn to fulfill their purpose in life, for each one of us is born with lessons to learn.

Not all spirits are Celtic Angels, as not all spirits want to interact with us. Indeed most spirits are indifferent to humans. Often I imagine these spirits as wisps of early morning mist lingering on the branches and leaves of a great ancient oak. The Celtic Angel is the spirit who appears to us either literally in a human form or whispers to us as we sit and meditate under the canopy of leaves.

Clearly the Celtic Angels cannot play the role of a heavenly messenger, as the Godhead is not an active God. Rather it is a passive repository of all our spiritual magnificence. Celtic Angels do have a role to inform and teach us of the existence of the Godhead and to awaken within us a longing to return. It is as if they can see it for us and translate some sense of the feelings of longing, of awe and of love that they feel. And perhaps by awakening this desire in our own souls, they remind themselves of their own need.

Celtic Angels are happy to play the role of guardian and companion. They surround us all the time and we can access their help and advice by simply asking for it. Celtic Angels, drawn from the realms closest to us, are useful because they have a real understanding and empathy with the human world and how it operates. These are the angels who are closest to us, and the easiest for us to reach.

Celtic Angels drawn from the second level of spirits that are beginning to look towards the Godhead are able to help us put issues into perspective and understand the appeals and attractions of both the spiritual and material planes. As they are beginning to disentangle from the material world, they tend to focus more on spiritual matters and can often have little sympathy with our own confused material longings. But sometimes that is what we need: a spiritual slap in the face.

Recalling the Buddhist belief that angels are bodhisattvas, enlightened beings who return to help others, Celtic Angels from the third level are those closest to and most aware of the Godhead. These Celtic Angels are the ones who truly inspire us and guide us along our spiritual paths. It is a great honor to be visited by one of those most noble of angels.

One unique aspect of the Celtic Angels is the existence of the Anamcara. An Anamcara, literally a soul friend, is a wise companion who never judges or condemns, who supports us and is always on our side. They are there to give advice and encouragement; they offer consolation when things go wrong and celebrate with us when we succeed. Because the angelic levels are not rigid, it is impossible to know precisely which level an angel is from, and an Anamcara may be drawn from any of the levels.

The Anamchairde (plural form of Anamcara) are mentors and teachers, friends and companions. It is an intense but most rewarding relationship, that will enrich your life and open you up to a whole lifetime of new experiences and discoveries. While it is very demanding it is also very fulfilling. Later on in this book, as you begin to work with your Anamcara, you will appreciate just what a precious gift it is to have an Anamcara and you will wonder how you could have been unaware of their existence in your life before.

What Do Celtic Angels Look Like?

Celtic Angels will normally appear in human form. However, like angels in the Bible, they do not normally have wings. They will appear in whatever form you find comfortable. There would be little point in them appearing like the Biblical cherubim with four heads, six wings and flaming swords: that would terrify anyone.

For me the angels always appear as male, but there is nothing inevitable about that. It may simply be that I find the image of old wise men more accessible than female forms. That said, my own Anamcara appears as a relatively young man with blond hair and an honest face. And he is always smiling.

As well as our Anamcara and other individual angels, we are surrounded by a whole choir of Celtic Angels. These angels change from time to time and rarely do they show any personality. They are attracted not so much by us, as by our spiritual energy. Adomnán in his biography of St. Columba tells us that St. Brendan saw a column of light shining from the great man's head.

For a while I was aware of these angels but, as they took no form, I could only sense a presence. That first night when they appeared at the river, they each did so by taking on the form of a sculpture that I had seen. They were small, with stylized triangular wings covered in Celtic knots. This image has stayed. It is pleasing and also anonymous. What I see is many identical images of this sculpture and even when the Celtic Angels move about the image doesn't change. Remember that all that is happening here is that our mind is selecting an image to let us "see" these Celtic Angels.

CHOOSING HOW YOUR CELTIC ANGELS APPEAR TO YOU

Take some time now to consider what the Celtic Angels will look like to you. Remember that they will appear different to every person. It is your subconscious that is making them visible. Seek out ancient books such as the *Book of Kells*, or some modern artists have images that might inspire you. Take as much time as you need and try to be open to ideas that seem to come from outside yourself.

Now, without actually deciding on an answer, consider the following questions:

a. Are your Celtic Angels male, female or androgynous?
b. Do they have wings, Celtic stylized wings or no wings at all?
c. Are they wearing tunics, robes or uniforms?
d. Do they show any sort of age?
e. Are they carrying anything?

Sit quietly somewhere you feel comfortable and think through all the images you have seen and the questions above. You will either find yourself drawn to an image or else a new image may form in your mind.

Do not worry if nothing happens right away. When the image is required, it will appear to you. All we are doing here is preparing for that moment, getting your mind to start thinking about it.

If you get an image in your mind or even just the shadow of an idea, jot it down in your Angel Journal. Try sketching it if you can. It will surprise you how quickly your image of the Celtic Angels will develop into a fully visualized being.

Celtic Angels do not have names. There is no need for them. For us it is all but essential. We have a real need to name everything in order to give some coherence to our thoughts and memories. When you meet your Anamcara you may, if you wish, ask for a name. That name will have some special resonance for you. You should try to keep this name secret, though working with your Anamcara is so intense and rewarding that it is almost impossible not to want to share your experiences with your friends.

The Angelic Agenda

Traditional Christian understanding of angels is that they are created by God to carry out His wishes. And so angels, while having free will, are nonetheless agents of a greater force. For Celtic Angels that is not true. There is no active God dictating actions, so they are free agents able to do and say whatever they want. Except that these beings are more spiritually advanced than we are. They have lived through all that we have and so much more, and so they have no desire to do anything but help us.

Each one of us is born with a lesson to learn. Our soul, our divine spark, chose to be born when it did; to parents and at a time and place that it wanted. All because it believed that the coming together of these different factors were most likely to create the situations to let it learn the lessons that it felt it needed to learn. Those lessons may be about self-worth, relationships, obsessions, attractions, behavioral characteristics or a million and one other factors. There may even be more than one trait or desire that needs to be embraced.

We are probably, at best, only vaguely aware of the needs of our divine spark. Even the lessons being learned may not be obvious. After all, if it was as straightforward as that, we wouldn't take a thousand lifetimes to learn. Celtic Angels can help us to work through our needs and may even assist us to be able to appreciate the experience.

That is not to say, however, that they are not able to plan and create schemes for the greater good. St. Patrick, for example, when he was looking for a site for a monastery on the Welsh coast, was told by angels that the site he had found,

Menevia, was indeed a powerful spiritual site, but it was designated for another. Within a hundred years St. David had built his own monastery there.

So our angels do have a bigger plan. And it is important that we accept that. After all, each one of us is only one of five billion humans seeking enlightenment, even if some, or even most, of them do not yet realize it.

A simple example of how angels can work together for our benefit is that they may suggest we go somewhere and there we meet a friend we haven't seen for a while, who in turn was influenced by his angels to walk a different way home from work. Or at a party we find ourselves literally bumping into someone else with whom we end up having an interesting conversation, or more. How many couples do you know who have met almost by chance? Maybe one of them wasn't planning to go out that night but changed their mind at the last moment. Or one of them was delayed for some reason and so they met each other on a train or waiting for a bus. Sometimes it feels as if the likelihood of any two people meeting and falling in love must be millions to one. And indeed that would be the case were it not for our angels.

HAVE THE ANGELS BEEN WORKING FOR YOU?

Sit down and take out your Angel Journal. Light a candle and say your invocation. Think back over your life and see if you can remember times when the angels were working for you. To begin with you might find this hard as so often we are completely blind to their work. Even thinking back, we seem to block out our appreciation of their influence in our lives. Of course that may be deliberate. However, think of people you have met; pleasant things that have happened to you and your family; accidents that were narrowly missed; sudden ideas that gave pleasure; birthdays or anniversaries remembered at the last moment. Now write them down.

Once you start, it is amazing the number of occasions you will discover where the angels have been with you. Their whispers and administrations have made your life so much better. And yet you never even noticed!

Now is the time to say thank you.

Look at each of the examples you have written down and take some time to remember as much as you can about the incident. Remember your emotions and how you felt at the time. Remember your hopes and dreams. Remember your pleasure.

When you are ready, say aloud, "Thank you, my angels. Thank you for making my life better and for being with me, even though I never realized it." Concentrate on these words as you say them and think about their implications. Say them with an intensity and love that you do indeed feel. That love will please the angels.

It is the nature of my work that I travel a lot. I remember one time when we were driving home, towing a trailer. Both the car and the trailer were piled high with stock from a complementary therapy health fair that we had been running. The trailer began to fishtail on the freeway. At first, I managed to keep control but then it started to fishtail again.

The trailer was beginning to swing from side to side. Then it was dragging the car with it. As we were pulled from behind, I wrestled to take control.

Suddenly I remembered somebody once telling me that the only way to recover was to speed up. Every instinct is screaming at you to slow down but the voice in my head was insistent. We had to speed up. I tried.

But it was too late! The trailer was now swinging wildly from side to side. With a sickening thud in my stomach, I realized there was nothing I could do. Nothing but wait for the inevitable crash.

Seconds later, we ended up on the hard shoulder facing the wrong way with the trailer on its side and the car slammed hard into the crash barrier. Yet we both walked away from it without a scratch. It was only too easy to see how it could have been so much worse.

Later, we realized that the accident was a real wake-up call. Until then we had "made do," dangerously overloading the car. We had been so lucky!

If we had to have an accident, this was the way to do it. Even our dogs, who always traveled with us, had for the very first time stayed with a friend that weekend. Now I thank my angels for teaching me so clearly that I needed to value my life and that of my partner.

FOUR

Celtic Angels and the Druids

Today there are many books on Druidism. You can attend classes; international federations exist; and a hundred different groups await you. Yet the original Druids, the religious leaders of the ancient Celts, wrote nothing down. They believed that the truths they taught were too powerful and precious to be confined to pen and paper. So all their understandings and practices have been more or less lost to us. All we are left with are folk memories, legends and place names to remind us of what once was.

This is to detract nothing from the modern Druids. Like their ancestors, they base a lot of their work on what they see and experience in the world today. Perhaps it is best to say that they are inspired by the example of the earlier Druids. And by joining them or working with them you can appreciate much of the mystery and magic of Druidism. It may well be that by so doing you will come as close to the original Druids and their practices as customs, laws and outlook will allow.

So we have to be honest and admit that our sources on the ancient Druids are very limited and inadequate. Most often we have to rely on material written by their enemies, as for example Julius Caesar, writing prior to his genocide against the Gauls of France. He paints a picture of a society dominated by Druids who practiced human sacrifice and lived in a twilight world of black magic, murder and fear. But then Caesar wanted to portray the Celts as primitive savages who were to be liberated from their ignorance and then civilized by the Romans. Before, presumably, seeing their leaders being thrown to the lions in Rome's Coliseum for the edification of the paying public.

A later source are the ancient tales and stories transcribed by the Irish Christian monks and nuns. From the sixth century A.D. onwards a large amount of oral material was translated on to paper by these most devout of men and women. Indeed it can be argued, and has, that while Western Europe fell into the Dark Ages, it was the dedication of these Celtic scribes that kept a candle of light and civilization burning across Europe.

Be that as it may, they nonetheless had their own agenda which means that we, today, find some of the work confusing and even contradictory. They could not, for example, accept that there could be gods and goddesses save the one True God. So many of these deities were transformed into Tuatha dé Danaan: fairy folk. A'ne was a goddess associated with health and healing and she became the queen of the fairies in some of these tales. These fairy beings could in turn be marginalized and eventually turned from real living creatures into mythical, half-remembered childlike beings.

It would, however, be too easy simply to dismiss these tales written by the Celtic Christian monks. Some writers have speculated that the Druids converted en masse to Christianity because they could foresee how impossible it would be to stand up against the Roman Church and its armies. If that was the case, they may have sought to protect their own sacred sites and deeply held beliefs by creating a veneer of Christianity to hide the deeper truth. Hence the sixth-century St. Columba could call Jesus Christ his "Chief Druid" without it being considered blasphemous by either pagans or Christians.

But this integration only helped to confuse matters further. If, for example, a local well is dedicated to St. Brigid, this may, or may not, be a Christianizing of a site dedicated to an older goddess. On Iona, Adomnán tells us that in times of drought, the monks would walk three times round a newly planted field with St. Columba's relics. They would then shake St. Columba's very own tunic three times in the air before retiring to the Fairy Hill, now renamed by Adomnán as the Hill of Angels. There, "where once the citizens of the celestial country were seen descending to talk with the blessed man," the monks would read aloud from the sacred texts. Almost at once, St. Columba's biographer reports, they would be rewarded with a plentiful supply of rain and in due course a bountiful harvest. We can only assume that this ceremony is an adoption of an older Druidic rite.

In this chapter we are going to examine the world of the Druids. In particular we will look at how they worked with the Celtic Angels. Finally, we will return to the great Irish sagas and show how, with a little careful reading, the presence of the Celtic Angels can be shown to be a lot more extensive than might at first be imagined.

The Age of the Druids

The Druids dominated Celtic Society for at least 1,000 years up to around A.D. 450. Like the Brahmins of India, they were more or less a separate caste. Membership was drawn from all sections of society but the leaders would almost certainly be from the same royal family as the local king.

Each kingdom would have its own Druids. Just like the later Christian monastic families, there may well have been many common links and even close contacts between the different Druids but each tradition would have varied in how they were organized, what they taught, how they lived their lives and the role they played within the wider clan.

Druidic training took up to twenty years. Because it was not permitted to write any of the teachings down, everything had to be committed to memory. All trainees had to be able to recite, word-perfect, huge amounts of poetry and stories or sagas. It is almost certain, however, that they did know how to write. Some archaeological finds in central Europe indicate that writing in Greek and Latin was common, but it would only be used for mundane day-to-day matters, such as trading with other peoples.

The Druids taught about astronomy and the nature of the earth, natural philosophy and their own gods. Almost certainly they would also teach about other religions, other languages and the use and abuse of herbs and other healing and mind-altering substances.

Although there is little archaeological evidence to back this up, it seems highly likely that the later Celtic monastic tradition of living apart from the rest of the people is derived, at least in part, from the Druids. There would have been one or more camps, probably with temporary wooden buildings and placed deep in the woods. The Druids may well have led semi-nomadic lives and the camps would be abandoned and reclaimed by the forest as they moved on.

There is no evidence for widespread accumulation of wealth by these Druid families. Of course we may simply not understand, or may be interpreting wrongly, the evidence that is available to us, but it would seem that the Druids scorned material goods and probably led severe, ascetic lives.

That said, these men and women were the most powerful in the Celtic lands and controlled all aspects of life. Even the

King had *gessa*, or taboos, placed on his actions by the Druids. They were his advisers; they were the law-givers and interpreters; they were the poets and news-providers; they were the historians and almost certainly controlled trade as well.

TREES THAT INSPIRE

The Druids recognized the spiritual importance of trees. Take some time now to appreciate the same qualities.

Seek out some ancient trees near you, perhaps in a city park or nearby forest. As you approach the tree, consider how you feel. Would you feel comfortable sitting under it? Do you sense any barrier or is the tree welcoming you? If you feel nothing or are not sure, walk on. Maybe rest on a park bench for a few minutes and then seek out another tree.

You will know when you have found the tree for you. There will not be a single doubt. You will appreciate its beauty and be aware, at once, of its welcoming nature.

Take some time to sit or stand under the tree. If you can, place your hand on the trunk. As you stand there try to empty your mind and simply let your thoughts flow gently along. Daydreaming is such a pleasant way to spend some time and yet we do so little of it.

Later, write down any thoughts you had while you were standing there. See if there is anything unexpected or even a realization of the solution to a problem that has been bothering you. You will be surprised how easy it is, in a tranquil place like that, to open up to the Angel Whispers—the voices of the spirits that are all around you.

Different trees engender different kinds of emotions and awareness in us. Try to find out what kind of tree it was that you were drawn to. There are many books now that explain what different trees stood for to the Celts. Find out what you can about your tree and try to understand why you were drawn to it.

Druid Teachings

We have little reliable evidence on what the Druids taught and what form their ceremonies took. It is known that they worshiped in the open air. They seem, in particular, to have favored working with trees. In Lucan's *Pharsalia*, written in the second century A.D., there is talk of Druids who live in the darkest groves and of how Julius Caesar himself ordered the destruction of a sacred wood at Marseilles in the south of France. Classical writers paint pictures of dark and gloomy woods, strange carved shapes of gods and goddesses and of blood splattered on every tree, carcasses hanging from hooks. Whether this sinister, forbidding world is true or not we have no idea, but it seems unlikely. Certainly the Irish sagas give no mention of this kind of activity.

At Pontfaen Church on the Pilgrims Way through the Gwaun Valley in North Pembrokeshire in Wales, the story goes that here, in the sixth century, St. Brynach was forced to flee from evil spirits that taunted him at night. The church itself sits on a small flat plateau surrounded by trees and looks down into the narrow, dark, heavily forested valley through which the small river winds.

The day I was there the air was still, almost unnaturally so. The church site was most probably a druidic one and I was drawn to an old yew tree on the very edge of the territory. There was indeed something unsettling about the tree. I had to force myself to approach it. It even looked threatening with its dark bark and poisonous needles. Not a tree to give you pleasant dreams. And I wondered if St. Brynach stood under this same tree or one of its ancestors and felt the same way. Of course there is nothing evil about a tree. It is simply that sometimes the energy it gives off triggers in us feelings of unease or dislike. We need simply to respect that and, like St. Brynach, move on.

The visit to that church made me realize how easy it would be for detractors to construct stories about dark and dastardly deeds deep in the forest. They would be able to use imagery that the average person would be able to appreciate: evil yews, dank alders and impenetrable blackthorn. Even to the average Celt the druidic sites were probably places of mystery. Druidic rites were rarely shared with the general population. Perhaps once a month there might be a ceremony; the rest of the time the Druids would conduct their strange practices in secret.

There appears to have been no fear of death. Warriors celebrated when one of their companions was killed, making them fearsome opponents. There are lots of stories of deals being struck in this world that were to be repaid in the next. This calm acceptance of death might have seemed sinister to some. Certainly Christians, taught to fear the judgement of St. Peter, found it hard to accept that we should welcome death. However, the Druids taught reincarnation. For the Celts life was a series of adventures that culminated in death. But death was not the end, merely an interlude before starting all over again in a new body and new time.

Druids also taught that in order to understand or appreciate anything we had to accept that there was not just a material side, but a spiritual side as well. If we feel unwell, for example, the cause of the malady may not be a physical one, it may be spiritual. Even today we talk of psychosomatic illness. Everything, the Druids taught, is surrounded by hundreds of spirits.

The belief in spirits meant that the druidic view of life was far more complex than what we are used to today. If crops failed or animals were sick, if the weather was poor or the warriors were defeated, this may have been caused by events in the spirit world, not our own. Druids, as healers, would be able to work with the individual angels of a person in order to heal them, the spirits being able to understand the cause of the affliction better than the individual themselves. Understanding the cause is the first step to cure.

The otherworlds, the world of the Tuatha dé Danaan, of the ancestors, of the gods and goddesses, and of the spirits, these worlds exist all around us. We, as normal humans, may even experience them in some way, but it was only the Druids with all their training who could walk these worlds and understand what was happening. It was only the Druids who could access these worlds in any meaningful way. And it was only the Druids who could plead, bargain, cajole and bully the beings in these otherworlds to make things better for the clan.

SENSING THE PRESENCE OF THE SPIRITS

It is estimated that there are over 3,000 sacred wells in the United Kingdom alone. Over 2,000 have been listed in the Republic of Ireland. Similarly, throughout the rest of the world there are venerated springs, lakes and pools. So you would be pretty unlucky not to live near enough one to go and visit it.

The purpose of this exercise is to sense the presence of the spirits or gods and goddesses that so inspired the Celts and the Druids in particular. Initially, do some research to try to find out as much as you can about the well. Your local library is a good place to start. There are extensive locally produced histories for most areas nowadays.

You should take a gift with you to the site. Tradition may state what that gift should be: sometimes it is a shiny pin or a piece of bread or a coin. If you cannot find out what to take, carry some white quartz pebbles with you and leave them at the site. Often there is also a clootie tree at the site. "Clootie" is a Scottish word for cloth or ribbon. The idea is that you tie a ribbon on to the tree so that even after you have left something of yours remains. On the road to Munlochy in the Black Isle, north of Inverness, Scotland, it has been estimated that there are at least 50,000 pieces of material on the tree. It has become a real eyesore!

At the well you should do your opening invocation. If it is too windy to light a candle, find some alternative that you feel comfortable with. You might drop a token into the water, or lay down some items from your Angel Altar.

Next you should follow any local customs that you have heard of that seem appropriate to you. If you have been unable to discover anything then you should sit by the well and dip your fingers into the water and sprinkle a few drops on the ground by the well as a token for the gods of the site. If you know the name of the god or goddess use it. If the site is named after a saint you may prefer to dedicate your actions to them.

Now sit and simply be aware of the water beside you. If it flows listen for the murmuring voices of the spirits that it reveals. If it is a pool feel the profoundness of its stillness. And enjoy.

And as your mind floats free, feel the energies around you. Try to sense any special feeling of presence. Welcome any awareness that this site is special. And share that moment.

Take as long as you want. When you are ready, make your closure ceremony and remember to thank the spirits of the site for your special experience. Then write down all that happened in your Angel Journal.

It may well be that you will find that you have to visit the site five or six times before you connect with the spirits. You should expect that. But that sense of being in the presence of special beings is well worth all the hard work!

Druids and Celtic Angels

Druids acted as advisers to kings. In order to understand better the issues on which they were being consulted, the Druids would often walk in the otherworlds, seeking help from the beings who lived there. Celtic Angels would act as guides for them, leading them along paths and perhaps even helping them should that be necessary. In many cases these angels would be the Druid's own Anamcara. But in other cases it might be angels who had particular attributes that the Druid needed at that point in time.

As advisers they would also be expected to prophesies. Again, while they would use their magic herbs and ceremonies, they would rely heavily on the Celtic Angels to see into the future and also to help them to understand what they were being shown.

Druids, as poets and storytellers, depended on inspiration from the otherworlds. It was believed that when a new poem was composed it was the whispers of the Celtic Angels that inspired the poet. Such was the veneration of these creative works that good poets would be held in awe by one and all, and a king was thought highly of if he acted as patron to these men and women.

In their day-to-day work, then, Druids worked closely with the Celtic Angels. As in the emerging Christian teachings, Celtic Angels were not worshiped. Rather they were companions and guides who would work with the Druids for the greater good. In so doing, of course, they revealed more of the nature of the spiritual world to these men and thus aided them in their own spiritual journey.

Celtic Angels and the Irish Sagas

It is clear from the material that has come down to us that the Celts were great storytellers. Modern scholars have analyzed these stories on many levels but naturally it is impossible for us to know how accurate the original written version is and how valid any interpretation can be. For most, the chances are that they were simply great stories told for entertainment and to glorify ancestors and clan history. However, because they can be understood in different ways it may be that there were indeed hidden meanings for those who wished to explore them.

One of the most famous of these sagas is the story of Diarmaid mac Aodha Sláine, a real High King of Ireland who reigned from A.D. 642 to 664. In the saga Diarmaid becomes infatuated with a woman and takes her to his capital to become his mistress. There she falls in love with his foster son. However, on her way in the early morning to meet him in a secret tryst, she is attacked by wolves and has to flee into the woods. There she discovers a handsome young warrior and follows him to an island. Despite the fact that he ignores her, she stays with him.

The next day she awakes to find a great battle between, on the one hand, her warrior and his three identical brothers and against them four fearsome warriors. The battle rages all day but ultimately is inconclusive and her warrior comes to her late in the day. He promises to return for her in a year if he is successful in battle. He then takes her back to Tara and no time has passed so she has not been missed by the King.

Exactly a year later he returns for her and Diarmaid, although he sees her leave with her warrior, orders them not to be stopped. A Christian ending has been added to this tale, saying that St. Molaise had a monastery on the island and had buried the seven dead warriors that very morning. Diarmaid ordered them to make a shrine and crosier for the monastery from the gold and silver of the men's accouterments.

While this can be seen as a tale of unrequited love and the generous heart of the King, there are clues that there is more to it than at first appears. The warrior's name was Flann, which means "scarlet" and this is the color often favored by beings from the otherworlds. It is also the description used for rowan berries, that most magical of fruit. The island's name was Fedach, "of the trees," and is seen as a reference to a pagan, pre-Christian heritage because the Druids often conducted their religious services in the deepest woods, yew tree groves being a particular favorite. This was a land of gods and magic. Beagfhola, the woman in the tale, then travels from the real world of kings and castles to this mystical world of heroes. However, it is possible to show Beagfhola as a form of angel, able to traverse the two worlds and to teach the worldly King about compassion and understanding. Her familiarity and longing for Flann and the mystical island reflect her own spiritual roots, while her motivation in the land of men seems solely to find love.

Of course some might be shocked to think of angels making love and beguiling men but remember the Book of Enoch, echoing Genesis, where angels come down to earth and take human wives. In other cases the role of the Celtic Angel is more explicit. When Cu Chulain, the great Irish mythical warrior, sets out with his war band to return an errant wife to the King, they are guided through the otherworld by a spirit.

So it can be seen that while the Druids were very powerful on the earthly plane, they nonetheless needed the support and help of the Celtic Angels, not only as they journeyed in the otherworlds but also as they sought to make sense of what was happening in this world. In the next chapter, on the Celtic saints, we will see how this tradition continues into the Christian era. For while we may categorize, codify and separate religious traditions, the Celtic Angels recognize nothing of this. For these spirits, their mission is to help us to understand and fulfill our spiritual goals. As we shall see, the gap between pagan and Christian is not as great as we, from our modern perspective, may think.

FIVE

Celtic Angels and the Celtic Monks

St. Brendan, born in the early sixth century in the west of Ireland, is most famous for his voyage when he set sail and may well have discovered America. And yet, when a Celtic Angel appeared to him when he was but a young man and pointed west out across the endless sea, St. Brendan could not understand what the angel was trying to say. It was only later, after more visits from the Celtic Angel, that he realized that he was being sent on a mission, a quest for the Land of Promise.

This Irish saga is one of the most famous today, not just for its beauty and narrative but also because it is so obviously an inner voyage of transformation and spiritual quest. As St. Brendan and his companions travel from island to island they meet strange peoples and creatures before eventually, in some versions, coming across Paradise.

For us the voyage of St. Brendan is reassuring, for it shows that even the most devoted of holy people have to learn how to work with their angels. It is not a skill that you are born with. As St. Brendan discovered, putting your trust in your Celtic Angel will lead you along the spiritual path you need to follow but, as each adventure unwinds, we still need our knowledge and experience to overcome each hurdle successfully and then carry on our way.

The Celtic Church

There is much we do not yet understand about early Christianity in the Celtic lands. The first Christians undoubtedly came with the Roman occupation of Gaul and Britain. True, there are legends of Joseph of Arimathea, and even Jesus Christ himself, visiting Glastonbury and establishing a Church there. In Scotland there are some who suggest that Jesus came to Fortingall in central Perthshire. This seems unlikely as these men, when they were alive, were not seeking to expand the faith beyond the Jewish population in the Holy Land.

It is more likely that as the Roman Empire embraced Christianity as its official religion in the late fourth century, state officials and those wishing to curry favor would convert to the religion of their overlords. There is little evidence that, after the Romans left in A.D. 410, the Christian Church remained in anything other than isolated pockets.

It is perhaps ironic then that when Christianity re-emerged in the Celtic lands it did so in the one part of the world that the Romans had not been able to conquer: Ireland. The first reference we have to Christians in Ireland is an instruction by Pope Celestine in A.D. 431 to Bishop Palladius to go and administer to "the Irish believing in Christ." A bishop was not sent to convert people so it suggests that it was believed there was a sizable community of Christians already there. It has been put forward that these people were probably slaves and ex-slaves captured by the Irish from the west of Wales. Whoever they were, Bishop Palladius' mission was a failure and he lasted less than a year before sailing north to Scotland. There he seems to have had a little more success but the evidence is patchy and uncertain, based largely on the survival of place names that may be associated with him, such as Aberfeldy, a corruption of "at the foot of St. Paddy's burn" or Aberpaldy.

By the time St. Patrick arrived in Ireland, probably in the middle of the fifth century, there were clearly some Christian communities in existence. Despite popular belief, St. Patrick was only one of many holy men and women who evangelized the Sacred Isle. Like St. Ninian of Scotland, St. Patrick's life is surrounded by myth and legend to the point that it is very difficult for us to know the truth. With both men we do not even know how closely they followed the Roman Catholic teachings.

Unlike the Church today, the Celtic Church was organized around monasteries where men, and often women too, would live and work worshiping God. These monasteries would send out monks to establish new daughter houses and gradually monastic families were established. There was no hierarchical Celtic Church, rather a series of these monasteries linked to the most prominent families and their allies. St. Columba, for example, eventually established his main monastery at Iona off the Scottish west coast. All the monasteries he established lay within the kingdom of Dalriada on Scotland's west coast and the patronage of his own O'Neil family. Later, as the Scots of Dalriada expanded and eventually linked up with the Pictish royal family, this monastic family was to become the Church of all Scotland.

In many cases monasteries were built on old Druid sites. Like the Druids' halls before them, the original churches were made of wood. They would be surrounded by small stone cells built by the monks themselves. There would also be a cookhouse, stores and possibly a meeting house. A couple of guest huts would complete the monastery. St. Blane's on the small island of Bute in the Firth of Clyde is an excellent example of a small Celtic monastic site. Originally it was almost certainly a retreat for, presumably, St. Blane from the much larger monastery about a mile due north at Kingarth. Over time the site grew to what we can see today: around twelve tiny stone cells for the monks to sleep in, the remains of a church and a cashel, or turfed low boundary wall, to mark the territory. The immediate impression is how tiny the site is and while it is quite sheltered on a southerly slope, nonetheless it is remote and it is difficult to imagine that the monks could grow many crops there. It is estimated that the monastery was in use until the twelfth century.

Sites were chosen with great care. Often the saints would be guided to a spot by their Celtic Angels. Of course some sites were more popular than others. One legend tells of St. Columba, exiled from Ireland, racing St. Moluag to claim the island of Lismore at the foot of the Great Glen. Realizing that he was losing, St. Moluag cut off his little finger and threw it onto the island and cried out, "My flesh and blood have first possession of the island, and I bless it in the Name of the Lord."

In fury, St. Columba cursed him, "May you only have alder for firewood."

"The Lord will make the alder burn pleasantly," replied St. Moluag.

"May you have the jagged ridges for your pathways!"

"The Lord will smooth them to the feet," came the response.

And to this day, alder is the most common wood on the island and the shoreline is marred by near vertical layers of hard rock that are all but impossible to walk on.

St. Columba was forced to retreat and took possession of Hinba, another, now unidentified, island. Ten years later, presumably with the support of the Dalriadan king, he evicted the monks from Iona and established his own monastery there. Lismore, now eclipsed by Iona, was nonetheless one of the main centers of Scottish Celtic Christianity together with Applecross in the far northwest.

The Creation of Celtic Christianity

One of the puzzles of this time is how Ireland, and then the rest of the Celtic lands, converted so quickly and so completely to Christianity. At around A.D. 431, as we have seen, Ireland only had some isolated Christian communities in the south, yet by A.D. 500 (and probably much before this) the whole land had converted to Christianity.

Beyond a few isolated tales, there is no evidence of any widespread conflict between the Druids and the new Christian monks; there is no evidence of any social unrest or overthrowing of traditional elites. It is as if the monks replaced the Druids and everything just carried on as before. Even more remarkable than this is the fact that the records we have were recorded by the victorious Christian monks, so it was in their own interests to exaggerate their successes, but they don't. The only reasonable conclusion that can be reached is that the Druids, almost as a mass, welcomed and embraced the Christian way of life.

This is not as remarkable as it may seem to us now. We have already shown that the Celts were very pragmatic about their religion and were always open to new ideas and practices. There is some evidence that they would already have had knowledge of the practices of the Egyptian Coptic Church and so the teachings of the monks would not have been so alien to them. Again, as we have seen, the new monks took on the role and image of the Druids. They would have taught in the same places, celebrated the same festivals and lived a similar life to the Druids. Indeed, for the ordinary Celt there was probably very little obvious difference.

Understanding the importance of tradition and family to the Celt, the new Church made no attempt to displace the ancient gods and spirits; rather they were merely integrated into the new cosmology. There are many tales and sagas where St. Patrick would resurrect ancient heroes and convert them to Christianity. A curious variant on this theme is St. Patrick's attempts to convert the great warrior Ossian when he returned from the T'r nan Og, the Land of the Young, where he had lived for 300 years with the beautiful Niamh, daughter of the sea god Mannanán mac Lir. Now returned, an ancient on the verge of death, he listened to St. Patrick's tales of the glories of Heaven and horrors of Hell. He argued vigorously against the saint, however, rejecting his arguments that his former war band the Fianna would be in Hell. He would not believe that Heaven could remain closed to the Fianna if they wanted to enter it. Besides, he argued, what use is eternal life if there is not hunting or wooing fair women or listening to the songs and stories of the bards? He finished by saying that he would die as he had lived with the great war band of Fionn and the Fianna.

In a land where there was no formal pantheon of gods, and certainly no great omnipotent being, it would be relatively simple to reveal the existence of a supreme being to whom even the local gods paid homage. Equally, in a land where the Tuatha dé Danaan walked, gods and goddesses lived, and changelings were well known, the news that a god would have his only son born as a human was not as remarkable as might be imagined.

Celtic Monks, Angels and Anamchairde

From around A.D. 450 until around A.D. 850 the monastic style of living encouraged the emergence of the Celtic saints. These inspiring men and women were the spiritual descendants of St. Anthony and St. Philip, the Desert Fathers. Like them, their quest was for sanctuary and peace; their aim to leave the day-to-day world behind and to find spirituality in the silence and space between work and dreams.

We know of these remarkable people through some contemporary sources and also later hagiographies, often written to glorify the saint and attract pilgrims to their sites. Celtic hagiographies are full of stories of saints and angels. Indeed the miracles performed by the saints are quite remarkable. St. Columba, according to his biographer and successor as abbot at Iona, St. Adomnán, could change water into wine; raise the dead and had a miracle bow that always hit its target. It is too easy for us simply to dismiss these stories as wishful thinking. It may well be that these men, with their knowledge of herbs, folklore and magic, may have been able to perform acts that would have seemed like miracles at the time. Seeming to raise the dead, for example, would be possible if you realized that the person was in a deep state of unconsciousness and you knew how to use stimulants such as pennyroyal.

With the stories of the Celtic Angels, this is also true. Like Druids, is it not possible that these saints, who walked as much in the spiritual worlds as they did in the material ones, did indeed converse daily with the angels? When Adomnán says that St. Columba's cell radiated a golden light of angels, that might literally be true or it might be figuratively true where the monks beholding the scene would themselves be able to sense the incredible spiritual power that was present even if they did not literally see the golden light.

The oldest mention we have of a Celtic Angel is from St. Patrick's own writing. St. Patrick had a close and powerful relationship with the Celtic Angels. As a young man he was captured by the Irish and brought as a slave to northern Ireland. It was there that he rediscovered his Christianity. After he escaped it was an angel, Victoricus, who came to him in a dream and summoned him back. This angel was to stay with Patrick all his life. Muirchú, writing in the seventh century, tells us that the Celtic Angel came to St. Patrick every seventh day and "Patrick would talk and enjoy dialogue with him, like one human with another."

St. Senan of Scattery was born in County Clare towards the end of the fifth century. He too was famous for his close contacts with the angels. Indeed it was said that when his mother went into labor, she was on her own and it was a Celtic Angel who acted as her midwife.

Stories were told of Senan, the young man who worked alone and yet did the work of two. One night two robbers came to his village and went to the mill where he worked. There they saw Senan was reading aloud while another youth ground the corn.

Deciding to wait until one left, the two would-be robbers spent the night outside in the cold. In the morning they challenged Senan when he left the mill alone. "Where is the man who worked with you all night?" they asked, peering into the empty mill.

"There was no man there but I," he replied.

"But we saw two people there."

"I said no *man*." Senan smiled.

Then the robbers felt a strange presence just behind the young man. Startled, they both fell at his feet and asked forgiveness for the crimes they had been about to commit.

As well as undertaking general labor, Celtic Angels would act as advisers to the saints. St. David, who went on to become the patron saint of Wales, had his monastery at Menevia, now St. David's, the U.K.'s smallest city, which lies in southwest Wales. There, every day, he would converse with the Celtic Angels. Indeed such was the fervor and passion of these discussions that often the saint would have to bathe in cold water afterward to recover. It was said that often voices would be heard in heated discussion within the saint's cell and that even the novices felt re-energized when they walked past.

A curious point about these encounters is that we are rarely told what was discussed. The teachings seem to have been for the saint alone. Neither is there any tale of such discussions being reported back to the monastic community at large. Indeed in one tale, St. Columba warns his pupil Berchán not to visit him as he will have an angelic visitor. When the pupil disobeys he is roundly punished by the saint and bore the scar of his punishment for the rest of his life.

The idea that the discussion between the Celtic Angels and the saint were private is a sure sign that the Celtic Angel was acting as St. Columba's Anamcara. An Anamcara (literally "soul friend") was a counselor, teacher and confidant all rolled into one. Every monk had one. The most holy of men and women had Celtic Angels as their Anamcara. Today we are all able to enjoy this most special of relationships.

Celtic Angels as Helpers

Celtic Angels were also couriers! When St. Aeddan forgot his bell used to summon the faithful, it was brought to him by the angels who flew out across the Irish Channel to deliver it.

Angels escorted souls to Heaven too. When the founder of Lindisfarne, St. Aidan, died in A.D. 651, St. Cuthbert, then a young shepherd, saw "a stream of light from the sky breaking in upon the darkness of the long night. In the midst of this, the choir of the heavenly host descended to the earth and taking with them without delay, a soul of exceeding brightness, returned to their heavenly home." This vision of the soul of St. Aidan returning to Heaven convinced Cuthbert to seek the life of a monk. Adomnán, while researching his hagiography on St. Columba, interviewed two old monks in northern Ireland who remembered in A.D. 597, as young novices, seeing a bright column of white light far distant in the northeast on the night St. Columba died at Iona.

Often the angels would warn the saint in advance of their imminent death. With St. David, an angel interrupted matins to warn the saint. While the other monks fell to the ground,

St. David rejoiced. He died a few days later surrounded by his monks and many other saints summoned by the angel, on March 1, A.D. 589.

This angelic power of prophecy was not restricted to foretelling death, but had other uses as well. St. Gobnata, a popular sixth- or seventh-century saint from Munster in southern Ireland, was told by an angel that she would never rest until she came across a place where nine white deer were grazing. This she finally did at Ballyvourney in County Cork. This intriguing site, with its mixture of Christian and pagan symbols, was almost certainly a druidic site and there remains a sacred well now dedicated to St. Gobnata.

Celtic Angels, Monks and Us

Although they lived well over 1,200 years ago, the Celtic monks can still be a great inspiration. They reveal to us how, by seeking a more spiritual path, we can access the otherworlds that lie all around us. By doing this we in turn achieve a greater understanding of the whole universe in which we live.

In our normal day-to-day lives, if we do not see the spirit realms or feel their presence, most of us either do not think about them at all or else we dismiss them as unimportant. It is like wearing blinders. If a horse is scared, you cover its eyes so that it cannot see and instead of it becoming even more apprehensive, it calms down, apparently forgetting what it cannot see. And we seem to be like that as well. It is only through our own spiritual awakening that we even become aware of the blinders. And that of course is a crucial first step in removing them.

Celtic Angels are demanding creatures. They know what we are capable of. They also know only too well our frailties and weaknesses. We have no need to be ashamed or embarrassed in front of them. Your angels love you and they want you to succeed. And no matter how often you stumble, wander off or fail, they will always be there for you; always willing you on and always on your side.

Take inspiration from the tales of the Celtic saints. Even today they have the power to inspire and motivate us. The memory of these most remarkable men and women shines down the centuries showing us the way.

And you will succeed. You will find your spiritual path. You will become aware of the spiritual realms and the magic that lie all around you in the land, the natural world and our fellow humans. And remember, it is not so hard, it is not so demanding.

Even as you read this, your Celtic Angels are already gathering. And, standing nearby, your Anamcara patiently awaits. The time has come. You are ready, eager and willing. So let's proceed! Your Celtic Angels await!

PART TWO

Working with Your Personal Celtic Angels

SIX

Preparing to Talk

There are many dramatic stories that show us that our angels can reach from the spiritual realms into our own world. Doreen Virtue, one of the United States' foremost writers on angel lore, tells of how she first truly became aware of the angels. She had felt them around her for a while but had ignored them, even when they warned her that she was about to be attacked and her car stolen.

This, of course, came to pass and the angels then told her to scream as loud as she could. This time she did listen to them and did as they said. Her screams alerted a passerby whose arrival on the scene scared off the potential carjackers. The aggression shown towards her left her in no doubt that her life had been in danger, and from that time on she paid more attention to the advice of her angels.

To have your Guardian Angels act like this to keep you alive must give you a great sense of impending achievement. You must feel there is a real purpose to your life that you have not yet fulfilled. And while there are many stories of this kind, this is not the most common form of contact between us and our angels. Normally it is far more subtle.

In this chapter we are concerned with revealing the gentle contact that already exists between us and our angels. Recognizing this is the first step in deepening and strengthening that link until, ultimately, we create a long-term continual relationship with our Celtic Angels. To do this, we need to reach out to the angels just as much as they reach out to us.

We Are All Surrounded by Spirit

The village of Lastingham nestles in the southern edges of the Yorkshire moors in northern England. It is a beautiful, gentle village graced with a small, traditional, gray-stoned Spartan church which seems perched on top of a round mound of grass. In fact this is an ancient holy site dating back to druidic times. This church is remarkable not just for its simple holiness. It has a barrel-roofed crypt dedicated to St. Cedd, a Celtic saint of the seventh century. It is almost impossible to express in words the calm serenity of that site. It has a sense of the divine that is precious. Precious because it is a place where you feel the spirits are at peace, content and smiling. To sit there on your own with a single candle lit is to grasp not only the truth that we are all surrounded by spirit, but to appreciate what that phrase actually means.

When you meditate in the crypt, you can feel the ancient powers all around you and you have a strong sense of not being alone. Perhaps most surprisingly, as you sit there meditating, you begin to understand that a part of you is spirit as well. Somehow you feel a connection, an affinity with the spirits who are already there in the sanctuary. And it may be this that is the most remarkable aspect of this site.

For the Celts, the world of the spirits and our own world were interconnected: there was no there and here; no them and us. This is because they recognized that humankind can play a special role in the world. We are probably one of the few, if not the only, beings on this planet who can be aware of our physical and spiritual bodies. In other words we are more than simply flesh and bone.

If our body is a car, then our mind is the driver and our soul, our divine spark, is the passenger. And, like any driver, our mind can ignore the passenger or pay attention to it. But it is our soul that reaches out to the angels who surround us all the time and so the more attention we pay to the divine spark, the easier and more fulfilling it is to work with the angels.

Already in this book we have shown you many exercises that allow you to feel the opening up of your spirit and an awareness of its needs and desires, as well as how it can inspire and enrich our lives. This has to be an ongoing process. We need that stimulation for us to be able to talk of a healthy soul, a fulfilled soul, a nourished soul.

A CONVERSATION WITH OUR SOUL

Imagine if we could talk directly to our soul! We can't because it is too integral a part of us. But what if we could? What would it say to us?

Light a candle and say your invocation. Sit quietly and feel the tensions of the day slowly flow from you. Feel yourself relax. When you are ready, look at the candle and watch the flame gently burning. This is how I visualize my own soul, a small flickering flame deep inside me, inside my heart. Close your eyes and try to see your own soul flame.

Would it be large, pale golden orange and healthy or would it be dim and deep red, barely visible in our day-to-day lives?

How do you feel when you look at that flame? Are you chastised for ignoring it, or do you feel appreciated and thanked for tending it with love and care? Does it feel eager to lead you on to new spiritual adventures or is it tired and apathetic, wanting only to be left to its own solitude?

What we are doing with this exercise is letting our innermost knowledge come forward to our own level of consciousness. Deep inside we know what we must do. We know our own needs. It is only our conscious mind that gets in the way. We are, if you like, fooling our conscious mind. But it works. You will come to understand things that you realize with a start are true of you: emotions you have suppressed, desires you have ignored.

The exercises in Part One of the book were designed to show you ways in which you can nourish your soul. Some ideas were frivolous, some fun, some challenging. Take your Angel Journal and write down, without checking, all the exercises from Part One that you can remember doing.

Now think back to the ones that you felt particularly drawn to. Make a plan in your Angel Journal to go through these exercises again over the next week. You might even come up with some of your own! Listen to your soul. After all, you can only have a conversation if both sides listen to each other!

When you are ready, slowly withdraw from your contemplation of the flame and return once again to your surroundings. When you feel comfortable, do your closure ceremony.

Protection

For the Celts there was nothing evil in the spirit world. It is only in later Christian-influenced texts that we begin to see mention of Hell or demons. The Celtic god Cernunnos, Lord of the Forest, King of the Animals, was demonized as Lucifer when the Catholic Church turned away from nature worship. This was their response to the continued attraction of such figures throughout history. Cernunnos is the stag that runs free; he stands for the untamed, wild part of all of us and was an energy, an archetype that the Catholic Church could not integrate into their structures as they did with so many other Celtic gods and goddesses.

However, despite there being no evil spirits out there waiting to entrap our souls, there are dangers that need to be guarded against. The main problem is that we need to be able to keep control of when we access the world of spirits and when we don't. For the ancient Celts there was no problem here as they often walked between the worlds; for us in the modern age, we do not have that luxury. Clearly, for example, when we are driving we need to be totally aware of where we are and what is happening around us.

There are many ways to protect yourself. I have found that the simplest is to have a gesture that you use to start spiritual work and another to close it. It has already been suggested that you light a candle to open your spiritual work. All this ceremony does is announce to yourself and the spirits around you that you are about to begin spiritual practice. Some people like grand gestures: circles of salt or casting of corn. Others recite prayers or poems. Whatever you feel comfortable with is the only guide here.

This protection also means that you are always in control. You can end the session at any time. If you feel uncomfortable with what is happening, or if something just doesn't seem right, simply close the session down.

Seeking Inspiration: Finding the Angels around You

We all need reassurance that what we believe is happening really is. It would be lovely if our Celtic Angels would walk into a room and tell our friends who they are. However, such events are rare as most of the time people are not thinking about spiritual matters. I often imagine Celtic Angels as conductors walking up and down the aisles of a crowded train, but with everyone too busy reading the papers or talking to each other to notice.

One very special occasion happened to me in the local church in the village near where I live. The church itself dates back to the seventeenth century, though most of the fittings are far more modern. The site, however, is ancient and has a gentle calm that I find most refreshing. I had gone along with one of my neighbors. While I attended church regularly at that time, she went only occasionally.

We were sitting in the pew side by side. The minister was giving his sermon and my mind had wandered off down dusty country tracks. Suddenly my awareness was called back to the now. It seemed to me as if there were an almost imperceptible stir in the air and it felt as if a huge angel wing had flowed over and through me. It was a most glorious and serene sensation: sad and happy in the same emotion. My neighbor began to cry softly and gently. Afterward she confirmed my feelings.

These confirmations by others of our own perceptions are very precious to us. Celtic Angels can use other methods too to remind us that they are there working with us. Often when I am out walking in the hills, I will see shapes that look like angels. One night I was convinced that there was a Celtic Angel standing by the side of a wall. On further investigation, I could see it was merely the shape of the boulders. When these things happen, it is the Celtic Angels whispering to us, reminding us that they are there.

Celtic Angels will sometimes leave an essence of their power when they have been working with you in a particular place. Sometimes that essence is an energy that you, and others, can feel for days, even weeks later. Sometimes it is a scent. Often I will smell the strange, exotic scent of coconut that comes from gorse in full bloom in the early spring. I once told my Anamcara how much I loved that smell. Other people frequently smell lilies when angels have been at work. Look out for these precious aromas when you are going about your day-to-day life. Smile and thank the angels for that special moment.

There is a widespread tradition that angels will leave white feathers to remind us of their presence. One woman I know of found a feather tucked into a book of poetry she was reading. As she said, there was no way it could have simply found its way there. It was all the more special because the page it was marking contained a poem that gave her great comfort at that moment in her life.

Once you have met your angelic Anamcara, your soul friend, you will find that you will see them often in crowds when you are watching TV or movies. When you know their name, you will hear people using it far more than you ever noticed before. Partly, of course, this is simply because we are looking for them. It's like when you become pregnant. Suddenly the town is full of pregnant women. In fact nothing has changed, it is just that you are now noticing something that before had no relevance for you. However every one of these occasions is special to us. They remind us of our Celtic Angels, our Anamcara and the love and care that they shower on us at all times.

We can also inspire ourselves. As you begin to work with the Celtic Angels more and more, you will find that you begin to acquire angel artifacts: pictures of angels, angel statues, angel lapel pins. Nowadays you can get almost anything linked with angels, even angel scarves!

These items are good for us as they are constant reminders of our desire to work with our angels. Every time we see them it should prompt us to remember our Celtic Angels and what we had promised to achieve with them.

CREATING AN ANGEL ALTAR

An altar is a special place for us. It is a spot where we gather items that are particular to us and it can become a focal point in our spiritual work. In my house we have several altars: some are ones I meditate with; others are simply there to prompt me to think spiritual thoughts, inspire me or remind me of important events.

I do not have shrines to my Anamcara as that is not appropriate. You do not want to worship your closest Celtic Angels, you want to love and work with them. They are our friends, not our gods.

To create an Angel Altar, we need to bring together the five elements of any world: earth, wind, fire, water and ourselves. Along with the always present nature, they help to create a special spiritual place for us. A plant that flowers continually, like impatiens, is a good companion for your altar. You can have cut flowers if you prefer, which are lovely and bright, but I prefer living plants.

For earth you can have the soil in the plant pot. Or you might want to collect some sand from your favorite beach or a small rock from a hillside that is important for you. Wind is usually marked by incense, fire by a candle, and water by a small bowl of water from a nearby stream or river. If you prefer, you could use sea water.

Now you want to add some angelic images. They might be postcards of famous angel paintings, such as William Morris's *Vision of the Holy Grail* or John Duncan's *St. Bride*, or you might prefer one of the many sculptures or stained-glass designs that are available. There is no rule here, so long as it is something attractive and inspiring that reminds you of your desire to work with your Celtic Angels.

Consider carefully each item you place on your altar. Quartz crystal is a good addition, for not only does it represent gifts from the earth, it is also a most powerful energizer. Select a form of incense that will inspire you, something that makes the back of your skull prickle with spiritual understanding. An alternative can be the scent of a candle. The aroma of lilies is always associated with angel work. Even the color of the candle can help. Generally blue, silver or white are considered angel colors.

Intuitively you will know what is appropriate for you. Ensure, whatever you use, that you create an equilateral triangle with two candles to the right and left corners and the angel image at the furthest away point with a candle either behind or in front of it.

You may have found a sacred site where there is a powerful sense of the Celtic Angels. If you prefer to work there, in the open air, then what you need is to replicate the power of that triangle in front of you. In truth this can be done with many different materials: stones, pieces of wood (ash or alder would be good) or even some crystals you've brought from the domestic altar. It seems that the image of the equilateral triangle, pointing away from you, is a powerful aid for us as we work with the Celtic Angels.

The altar itself can look as much like a traditional altar as you want. You may feel more comfortable with something that looks like a small gathering of items rather than the high altar of a great cathedral. It is entirely up to you. Remember, however, that an altar needs to be tended. It is the focus of your spiritual work and so you should tidy it regularly and add and take away items as the seasons and your own moods change.

I have two vanilla-scented candles with a small crystal ball in between. Behind them I have a small stained-glass angel with a candle behind it. Two large crystals are on either side with a plant at the side with an ash catcher for the incense and a bowl of rainwater at the very front. Around all this has gathered some cards that inspire me and an abstract wood carving done by my father, which he thinks of as a cactus but to me has always been an angel with its arms open to me.

Angel Whispers

While we all aspire to a deep and powerful relationship with our Anamcara, there are many other Celtic Angels around us and we need to be able to listen to them as well. These spirits have wisdom and insight that can help us in the routine of our day-to-day life. All this, of course, is under the guidance of our Anamcara.

What we are trying to do here is to adjust our lives to be compatible with our growing spiritual awareness. There is no point in seeking to converse with our Celtic Angels if we then carry on with our career in the weapons business! However, not all the changes we need to make are so dramatic. The Celtic Angels can help us as we begin these small and subtle changes that will bring us more into "the flow." And as we do so, more coincidences, pleasant occurrences and incidences of "good luck" will happen to us.

Celtic Angels seek to communicate with us all the time. These are the whispers that we hear in our mind. Most of the time we are not even aware of them. When we do hear an Angel Whisper, we may erroneously call it intuition, or a hunch or even something that we "feel in our waters"!

The advice or information the Celtic Angels wish to impart may not be earth-shattering or life-changing. It may simply be advice on how to make someone feel better. I had an example of this recently when suddenly, without thinking about it, I had the notion to buy a small present for my partner. When we met up again, it turned out that the morning had not gone well and so my little present was much appreciated. And of course not only did my partner feel better, so did I!

Take a few moments now to sit and think of all the things that have happened to you in the last few days caused by you following your Angel Whispers. Initially you might imagine that nothing like that has happened to you. But think again. Remember that sudden thought that made you call an ill relative, that sudden idea to cut the grass a couple of hours before the rain started or the decision about what to make for dinner.

Maybe you found a parking space easily in a busy parking lot by sensing where there was a space. Parking in the small market town of Wetherby, near Leeds, on a busy summer's day, not only did we need to find a space, it had to be large enough for our big van. My colleague called on her angels for guidance and we immediately found the only space in the whole lot. As we locked the van, one local came up and told us it was uncanny how the space had come free just as we entered the lot.

At the end of each day write down the Angel Whispers that you listened to and what subsequently happened. You'll be amazed how often you have heard the angels talk to you and you were not even aware of it!

After a while you might want to write down the Angel Whispers that you didn't follow. Try to see the consequences of ignoring the feeling. I vividly remember one day when I had an urge not to go on to the freeway but to take the scenic route instead. Anxious to get my journey over, I argued with myself and instead turned on to the freeway. An hour and a half later I had traveled about a mile in a huge traffic jam. There are few things more frustrating than sitting in a traffic jam knowing that if you had only listened to your angels, you could have been home half an hour ago.

Often your Angel Whispers are not so obvious. At the end of the day, you might wonder why it seemed so important at the time. Perhaps, like the freeway hold-up, it is to avoid something. If I had listened to my angels and driven the other way, I might have called myself daft for adding time to my journey. In fact it would have cut almost an hour from the travel time.

Other times the whispers might encourage you to pick out a book you otherwise might have not bothered with; perhaps to think of a friend you have not seen for a while or maybe even spontaneously to decide to drive home a different way from work. The results of these actions need not be dramatic but remember you are being directed in some small way. And the more you listen to your Angel Whispers, the more magical and special your life will become.

LISTENING TO ANGEL WHISPERS

The more you practice this particular exercise, the easier it becomes. Take some time at the start of the day and sit quietly in a space where you feel comfortable. Light a candle and say your invocation.

Now think of the day ahead and all that you will be doing. As you slowly go through each stage of the day, see how you feel about it. For example, think of walking to the bus stop to catch a bus to work. Is there anything you should do before you leave the house? Do you get any sense that you should leave earlier or later than normal? Do you need to change your route?

To begin with you may feel nothing. Don't worry about it. As you do this exercise more and more you will begin to recognize the most subtle of feelings. Sometimes all I get is a sense that something doesn't feel right. For example, I work from home and, one day recently, I thought I would leave going into town to mail some letters until last thing in the day. Then I felt no, I should go earlier. I did this and met a friend, went for coffee and then returned to work more refreshed and energized than if I had plodded on through the day.

You may wonder how you know when it is a genuine Angel Whisper and when it is just wishful thinking. That fresh meringue, pie may look very tempting. You might think that your angels are advising you to eat it. But inside, if you are honest, you know that it is sheer greed that is propelling you through the door of the bakery.

If you feel that you are really being advised about a big decision, take some time; talk to friends and even take professional advice before making a final decision. For example, you might have a fabulous vacation in Florida and after you return you feel that your angels are telling you that you need to go and live there. Don't just act on that feeling: consult your family; try to find other people who have moved there and find out how they have fared. Consider how you would make a living. For all that it might be desirable from the angels' point of view, they don't have to pay utility bills or buy food. Perhaps it would be good for you to move but maybe you have to make compromises.

After you have been practicing this for a few weeks and feel relatively confident about working with the Celtic Angels, why not set aside a day to try to follow all your Angel Whispers? This is best done on a day when you do not need to be at work or doing anything in particular. You should find that you have a lovely day and go to bed refreshed and content.

There are many aspects to our life and the Celtic Angels can help us not just with the major decisions we need to make but also the smaller, more mundane matters. As we work more and more with the Celtic Angels, we begin instinctively to listen to their advice. And as we increasingly follow the path they lay out, the easier it will be for us to open up to the spiritual world. In the next chapter we will look at how we can reach out to these spiritual beings; how we can, in fact, talk to our Celtic Angels.

SEVEN

First Contact

Although the Celtic Angels are all around us, it takes time for us to "tune in" to them. While we may hear whispers and even sense their presence at a sacred site, that is merely a shadow of the strength of contact we can acquire. In this chapter we are going to look at how we can reach out to the Celtic Angels using dream work, visualizations and meditation. Then in the next chapter we will see how we can build on these initial contacts.

As we slowly develop our abilities to call out to the angels, we need to bear in mind at all times that they want us to succeed. They are eager for us to discover our spiritual potential, but they need us to work with them.

When I first started to work specifically with the angels, I was aware of a great period of change in my life. I had already been warned by the angels that as I worked with them and their energies, I would be affected quite profoundly. In fact I went through a short, sharp purge that seemed to cleanse my body and mind. During this period I felt submerged in angel teachings.

These spiritual beings use our language because that is all we understand, but in this intense period of change it seemed to me that image and shapes were more important. It was as if these means of communication were more real for the Celtic Angels and while I could not understand what I was being shown, at some level, perhaps some race memory, recognition and understanding did, I feel, occur. Some of this we will use later as we learn to communicate with our Celtic Angels.

As well as this purge, other changes happened too. Perhaps the angels were asking for some sort of self-denial from me to show my intent, I really don't know, but a lot of my favorite foods lost their appeal. Other changes also occurred: nothing drastic, just subtle changes of perception. If you experience this, it is nothing to be alarmed about. It makes sense that the angels will bring change with them. There would be little point in all this effort if the result was that our lives carried on as before.

Look for these kinds of demands for change as you set off on this path. In particular notice if you are drawn to specific colors. The range of colors that we are attracted to and wear or surround ourselves with can often indicate special needs or desires within ourselves. Blue and silver are the main spiritual colors. You may, however, find yourself drawn to other shades. This can be a way in which the Celtic Angels try to tell us of our own needs.

You may also feel desires to visit particular sites. These may be sites with an obvious spiritual connection, such as old churches, standing stones or holy wells. In that case try to find out as much as possible about the site and see what aspects of its history particularly resonate with you.

We were in Callander in the Trossachs in central Scotland and I was aware that there was a church there dedicated to St. Kessog of Luss, a man who has inspired me in much of my spiritual work. However, we could find no trace of it and, as I was there with others, I reluctantly gave up the search.

Back at the parking lot, I felt a strong desire to climb a small hill at the side of the river there. It looked like a mound of earth left from some landscaping work and sat, solid and dumpy, maybe ten feet in height. I decided I couldn't be bothered and it was my partner who climbed it and then called out to me. It turned out that the church had been demolished and this mound was where the church would have stood. I learned from this two important lessons. First, always listen to your angels and, second, do not give in to your expectations. I had expected a quaint small church like the parish church at Lastingham, not a mound of earth. Yet there was something about that site, something that resonated with me. It was difficult during a day with children playing and cars coming and going, but I do intend to return to experience the magic of the site one quiet night.

Using Dreams

Celtic Angels can reach out to us while we sleep. Their whispers influence our dreams. And in the morning all we need to do is to try to understand what message they were attempting to pass on to us.

Before you start doing any dream work, you need to begin to keep a Dream Journal. This should be a book you have by your bedside. First thing every morning write down all you can remember of your dreams. Do this before you talk to anyone, go to the bathroom or do anything that may interrupt your memories. If you sleep alone then you can do this during the night as well if you awake after dreaming.

You will quickly realize that you are dreaming a lot more than you think you are. When I was young I would often wake up and not remember having written down any particular dreams. Yet there, in the morning, would be pages of description. It gives you a strange feeling to see your own handwriting in the journal when you have no memory of either doing it or even the dream it describes.

It should take a few weeks before you are so comfortable doing this that you barely notice it in the morning. Reaching for the journal and pen just becomes an automatic response on waking.

It is useful to spend time later in the day trying to understand the dreams you have had. Sometimes talking to someone else can help. I often find that, as we swap our dream experiences, I remember more details of the dreams I've had. Frequently you can see references to things that have happened recently to you, TV or DVDs you have watched or even books you are reading at the time.

You will also begin to notice that certain items or places come up regularly. You need to understand what these places stand for. I have a coastline that I often visit in my dreams. There is a long sweeping bay with a café/restaurant at the far end. It was only by going over my dreams that I came to see that I only ever visited there when my parents were involved in my dreams. And indeed they do live by the sea, though not in such dramatic surroundings. When I dream of my own house, it is never as it is, but rather it has hidden rooms, old courtyards and outbuildings. Nonetheless I recognize that house in my dreams.

By all means refer to dream books to help to understand the symbolism of your dreams. However, you need to be aware that your own life experiences, and maybe past-life experiences as well, can affect how some symbols have to be understood. An obvious example is a dog. If you lived with dogs all your life, then a dog would be a positive symbol, perhaps relating to companionship, unconditional love or domestic family contentment. But if you were attacked by a dog when you were a child, then the presence of a dog in your dreams may be a far more threatening or aggressive symbol.

Sometimes you will also realize that you have dreams that have no relevance to anything else going on in your life. These dreams are the messages from our Celtic Angels. Take particular care with these dreams to seek to understand and act on what they tell you.

Dream Work

What few people realize is that we can influence our dreams ourselves. We can create environments, introduce characters and even direct whole epic scenarios if we so choose.

Before you go to bed light a candle and say your invocation. Create by your bedside a sacred space with the four elements and nature. If you prefer, you can burn your candle elsewhere in the house, perhaps in an empty fireplace. Write down in your Dream Journal who or where you want to dream of.

Once you get into bed you need to take some time to relax. As you lie there, concentrate on your breathing, focusing on how you breathe in and out. Feel the comfort of that slow regular circle of actions: gently breathing in and then slowly breathing out. In and out. In and out.

Notice how your breathing is slowing down, how each breath in seems slower and each breath out more gentle. Gradually, as you sink into that darkness that slowly cuddles around you, think of the person or place you want to dream of. Even your thoughts are getting soft and fuzzy. Pictures are getting difficult to keep hold of. Slowly you are drifting into a dark beautiful place. Keep hold of that image. If it drifts away, pull it back. And so to sleep. And to dream.

The easy way to start is with a person you know really well, perhaps a parent or partner. Don't be surprised if you succeed very quickly. You do however need to be able to do this almost at will before we can truly consider it a success.

Once you have succeeded in introducing characters into your dreams, try objects. In particular, any angel artifacts you have. If you have made an Angel Altar, a good exercise is to try to dream of sitting in front of it watching the flames on the candles. I have had many pleasant dreams of this.

For the Celtic Angels we can make it easy by setting the scene for them. You might want to imagine the opening scene for your dream. It could be a place where there is the most beautiful Angel Altar in a clearing, surrounded by tall, venerable oak and beech trees. The sun is shining and birds are singing.

The idea of creating your own dreams may seem fanciful to you. But consider your experience if you are going on vacation early the next day. Most of us do not sleep well the night before and spend most of the night in dreams where we are arriving at the airport without tickets, at hotels without suitcases or campsites without our children. Clearly whatever was worrying us as we went to sleep is influencing our dreams. These exercises simply allow us to create good things to have in our dreams instead.

Do not, at this stage, try to conjure up actual angels. That will come. What we are doing here is slowly pushing open the door. You may well dream of angels or spirits and that is fine but you do not want to force the pace. Let them come to you.

Even when you are totally comfortable with the idea of creating your own dreams, there will always be the odd variable that you cannot control: an ostrich that wanders across the garden; the dinosaur that rears up out of the placid loch; or the alien that sits and has afternoon tea with you. That, however, is the fun of dreams.

The Dream of Angels

There are many sacred sites associated with angels. Perhaps you know of one already. If you do, then for this dream exercise you need to imagine you are there. I use Croagh Patrick in County Mayo, Ireland. There, on the flat top of the mountain, you can sit facing west over the surrounding hills and the amazing Clew Bay with its mass of islands, many of them looking more like green basking whales than any sort of land. I choose this spot because it has a unique energy, an angel energy that can only be described as white. When I was last there it was very misty and with the huge bulbous clouds drifting past below and this white energy flowing around me, it simply lifted me to another angelic realm: a place of peace, subtle understanding and sense of connection with the spiritual worlds. It was as if I was there, on Croagh Patrick, and also in some other wonderful place. And it is that sense that I seek to conjure up in my dreams.

The purpose of this exercise is to give you the first glimpses of the angel world. You should make no attempt to contact them.

In your dream, imagine that you are at this angel site, either the one I've described above or one you already know. It is that soft light pre-dawn when everything seems clean and fresh and the sun has not yet begun to shine. The site is completely empty.

Now see the light beginning to turn a pale golden. The sun is rising over the horizon. Turn slightly and see it climb up as you watch. You know that when you turn back you will see the angel site as it really is, full of angels. When you are ready, slowly turn around.

It is an incredibly moving moment. It is so lovely to see. It is inspiring and exciting.

Stand and watch for as long as you want. When you are ready, close your eyes in your dream and feel a gentle, deep warmth wrap around you. Feel the darkness slip over you and then slowly drift back into a deep, satisfying sleep.

Using Visualizations

Unlike dreams, visualizations are something you do while awake. They are, however, in many ways like daydreaming or like listening to a story where you can "see" the narrative unfold. With visualizations you are normally led by another to a certain point in the description of an event and then you are left to see what happens next.

Like dreams they are something that you need to practice. Eventually you can make the experience so vivid that you can almost feel as if it were real. And certainly afterward I often have to think hard as to whether an event actually happened or if I visualized it.

A good way to start is to listen to some recorded stories. Books on tape or CD are available in most libraries and many bookstores stock an extensive range of titles. Although you can use them when driving or doing another activity such as ironing or mowing the lawn, it is best to listen to them while doing nothing else if you want to practice visualization skills. I remember one car journey as a passenger traveling north on freeways through the night. The book was John Wyndham's *The Day of the Triffids*. In the black-and-white world outside, as the anonymous cities sped past on roads that were almost empty, the story of man-eating plants that take over the world after everyone is blinded seemed just a little too real.

Listen to the book and then pick a scene that seems particularly vivid for you. It may be a description of a room or a walk through countryside that you know. It may even be of a person. Play that scene over and over, each time making the picture in your mind more and more vigorous. Success is when you can listen to that scene and not even hear the voice of the narrator, when it is lost in a picture so real, so vivid that you feel as if you are really living it.

Visualizations can take two forms. On my CD *Celtic Meditation* we have a track where we take you on a walk through a real wood at Grassington, near Skipton in Yorkshire. There you are led to various spots in the forest where the influence of the spirits and angels living with the trees helps you to see aspects of your life and how to improve them. This is a common form of visualization where, effectively, a story is being told.

Another form is where you are led along a path and then left alone. I was at a shamanic workshop where the facilitator used this form extensively, with great success. And that is the form I offer to you here.

VISUALIZATION TO FIND A GIFT FOR YOUR ANGELS

In truth your Celtic Angels require no gifts from you. However, it is nice to show an appreciation of them and also to offer a token of your determination to change your life to work with them to make your experience on earth more spiritual and worthwhile.

Although you can do this exercise inside, it is a good one to do outside in the open air. If you do, change the described weather to suit what you can feel. If it is cold, remember to wrap up warmly! Choose a spot that is special to you and where there are no sporadic sounds that are likely to disturb you.

Make yourself comfortable. Light a candle and say your invocation. When you are ready, close your eyes. Raise your arms to the heavens to make a "Y" shape: the classic Celtic prayer position. Feel the energy there. Feel it rush through your arms and down through your body into the ground. Hold that position for as long as you can, only being aware of the energy flowing through you.

When you are ready, still with your eyes closed, sweep your arms down in a half circle in front of you and now it is as if you are standing in a great stone circle. It sits on the top of a brown, heather-clad, rounded hill with similar hills all around. Between the hills there are steep valleys with winding streams and craggy gray granite rocks standing out defiantly from the browns and muted purple of the heather.

It is a bright autumn day and the sky is a pale watery blue. There is a slight chill in the air but you are warmly wrapped in a great gray cloak of protection.

The standing stones around you are huge monoliths that tower over you. Slowly move around and count the standing stones. Remember that number, it is significant. Now look carefully at the stone directly in front of you. Although there are no carvings on it, there are shapes in the stone that, with the shadow from the sun, seem to be accentuated. They seem to be half-formed heads and animals. Walk forward and look more closely at them. One motif in particular seems to stand out. What is it?

Study the motif. It may be a figure, an animal, a tree. It may even be a scene: hunters returning from a hunt; women weaving; gods being worshiped. You need to remember this, so take as long as you think you need. Here in the circle you are safe and will not be disturbed. You are totally alone and outside the circle nothing moves.

Eventually you feel the call of return. Step back into the middle of the circle. Pause, and then, when you are ready, sweep your arms up in front of you and as you do so, you will become aware once again of where you are standing. Listen to the sounds around you and take a moment to readjust before you open your eyes.

Blow out your candle, thanking the angels for their support. As soon as you can, draw the motif that you saw on the stone in your Angel Journal.

The next day try to understand why you were shown this particular image. If it is of a bird or animal, try to find out more about the Celtic myths and legends associated with this creature (a good book for this is *Animal Wisdom* by Jessica Dawn Palmer). The image will have been chosen for a reason. Your Celtic Angels want you to think in a particular way and they have chosen that image to trigger thoughts.

Now take a large sheet of paper. If you counted, say, fourteen stones, you need to draw fourteen fourteen-sided shapes on the paper. Try to make them as similar as possible. If you are good at this kind of thing, you might want to draw them in different perspectives as if some are facing you, some are on their sides, others are far away. Celtic Angels seem to be fascinated by this type of construct.

Now in each shape draw your motif. As you do so think of the lessons you have been taught. This drawing is your gift to the angels. You might want to keep it: put it on your Angel Altar or frame it and have it on the wall. At the next fire festival (see my book *Walking the Mist*, Chapter 10 for information on the Celtic fire festivals), however, offer it up to the Celtic Angels by burning it, preferably wrapped around some ash wood—the wood of the Celtic Angels. This is a traditional method of offering a gift to the spirits: taking something solid and turning it into smoke.

Using Meditation

There are lots of different forms of meditation. It can have many positive purposes: religious, health, relaxation, bolstering intelligence or personal awareness. But the one thing that all forms of meditation have in common is that they seek to take your awareness to another plane. The Celtic saints would stand up to their knees in the icy-cold loch water for hours on end, oblivious to their discomfort as their most powerful meditation and prayers took them to another world.

The saints, like the Druids before them, were seeking to make contact with the spiritual realms. By peeling away our awareness of the material world, we empty our mind and so hopefully make ourselves more susceptible to the Angel Whispers.

Nowadays we no longer know precisely what techniques the Druids or saints used. From their beliefs, however, we can be sure that the magic of the land would be an essential tool for them. To that end I have devised a form of meditation that I call Celtic Meditation. You can do this anywhere but it will be more effective in some places than others. To start with, practice it in your home. Once you are familiar with it you may want to try it in other places. Be aware that at sacred sites the effects can be very powerful. At Long Meg, near Penrith at the east of the English Lake District, the energy was so strong that as I brought the energy into my body it seemed to me that I grew and grew until it felt as if I had become a light being ten feet tall!

CELTIC MEDITATION

Find a place where you feel comfortable and will not be disturbed. Light a candle and say your invocation. Sit for a few minutes and then, when you are ready, plant your feet firmly on the ground and close your eyes.

Now imagine shoots, like tree roots, growing out from the soles of your feet down into the ground. Feel the power of the earth around you and slowly pull that energy into your body.

With each breath in, feel the energy of the earth being sucked up into your body. Little by little feel it rise into your feet, up your legs, across your stomach, down your arms and up through your head until you are totally a being of the soil.

Feel the cool certainty of the land. Hear the silence of the soil; smell the rich fertility of the earth.

Hold that feeling for about ten seconds and then, when you are ready, feel a rich shower of pure white light washing through you from the top of your skull, down through your head, shoulders, torso and down through your legs and into the soil. Feel the connection from the eternal white light of the angels into the rich dark power of the earth.

You are a being of the light! Rejoice!

Pull the power of the earth up through your body once again. Feel the soil rise; sense the connection to all living things around you. You are of the earth. You are of the land. Feel the contentment and love of the mother earth flow through you.

Hold that sensation of calm certainty.

As before, wash away this solidness with the delightful freedom of the white light. See yourself laughing and smiling as the shower flows through you. Feel your body cleansed and purified by the white light of love. Feel it fill up within you.

Hold that sensation of love and peace.

Now for the third and final time, pull the earth energy up through your body. Feel it rise smoothly through your legs and up your chest; down your arms and up through your head. Feel yourself a being of the land. Feel the cool dependability of the soil. You feel great!

Hold that certainty.

And once again the white light of the heavens flows down through you, washing all the earth energy away and replacing it with glowing white love. Feel your body fill up. Sense the energy flowing down feeding the land.

You are a being of the light! Feel the energy, the knowledge and the freedom all within you. Sense the energy beaming out of you. You are glowing! You are alight!

You are serene.

Hold those feelings and now just let go. Feel yourself float. You may literally feel as if you are levitating. Do not panic, this is a most powerful meditation and sometimes it feels as if not only our mind floats free.

You are now in a very special place, a place where the veil between the worlds is very thin. The energy that you are giving off will attract angels to you and you may feel their presence as they flow around near you. To them you are a powerful beacon of light energy.

Let any anxieties or worries that come into your mind drift away. They are of no importance as you embrace your spiritual being; they are so irrelevant to you that they simply evaporate like small fluffy clouds on a hot, sunny summer's day.

Hold that sense of freedom and contentment for as long as feels comfortable and then, when you are ready, prepare to return to your earthly awareness. Feel your body around you again. And, when you are ready, open your eyes. Take a few moments and then make your closing-down ceremony.

This is a most powerful meditation technique and you should take several minutes just to sit quietly before moving on. You may feel a little disoriented or even dizzy. Do not worry, that is perfectly understandable. Take your time. Have a stretch, look around and move your arms and feet.

Ideally you should aim to do this exercise daily. I do it at the start of the day, sitting out in the garden in the summer, kneeling in front of my shrine in the winter. I always try to face east, which I have found most effective, the same direction in which Celtic churches were positioned.

When I visited Lindisfarne on the Holy Isle, just off the Northumbrian coast in northeast England, I was very impressed by the presentations on the Celtic church first founded there in A.D. 634. However, as I sat and meditated in the small stone church there was no real sense of presence. Disappointed, I sat back and considered the lie of the land. Was I perhaps not in the spot that the early missionaries would have chosen? But there was nothing to suggest that this was not the spot. There was no obvious alternative.

Then it came to me: the pews in the church were facing the wrong way. Twisting around in the narrow seat until I was facing what I thought was east, I tried the Celtic Meditation again. This time, like a homing beacon, I sensed an energy and as I adjusted the way I faced even more, I felt a great gentle wave of love sweep over me. To myself I called this energy St. Aidan, after the founder of the Northumbrian church. It was delightful, all the more for being unexpected.

Celtic Meditation is the basic meditation technique and we will be using it extensively in this book. You may feel at first that it seems rather cumbersome and time-consuming. However, you will quickly become comfortable with the technique and in fact you can do the whole exercise in a few minutes. For myself, I prefer to take my time and enjoy all the different sensations. The beauty of the exercise is that it connects us to the magical energies of the land and the spiritual worlds and helps us to move to a place where we leave behind the boring, humdrum material world and open ourselves up to the exciting, loving world of the Celtic Angels.

EIGHT

Conversations with the Celtic Angels

We have already recognized the importance of Angel Whispers, these ideas and messages that we pick up on. Now, in this chapter, we want to develop contact with our Celtic Angels a bit further and begin a conversation with them. Many Celtic Angels will gather around you but only one or two individuals will come forward and work with you. The others, simply by their presence and interest, offer you support and well-being. Occasionally when the time is appropriate you may find one or more of them approaching you. Normally, however, they are content merely to be with you.

Why do you want to talk to your Celtic Angels? This question was first posed to me at an old temple site I visit near my home in East Lothian. When visiting sacred sites, I always feel that the journey is almost as important as the site itself. And so as I was walking along the sacred path that winds around the side of Doon Hill, I was attempting to keep my mind empty except for the sounds of the wind and the beauty of the bushes and young trees that surrounded me. Suddenly from nowhere a voice filled my head. At first I thought someone had spoken to me, though I knew that there was no one else around. Why do you want to speak to the Celtic Angels? The question seemed to fill my whole mind and hung there, gentle yet perceptive, as I struggled to think of an answer.

You can have no secrets from your angels and so it always pays to be upfront and honest, as they will cajole and encourage you until you admit the least attractive parts of yourself. So I will start by saying that I concede that there is an element of glamour, of excitement and of thrill of working with the occult (i.e., hidden) energies.

For many people I suspect that is an honest and frank answer. You do get something of a buzz from the idea of being able to converse with an angel. Not only is it something that many people believe only a few can do, having such a skill reinforces the idea that you must be special, more spiritual or chosen in some way.

In fact, conversing with angels is a bit like learning a foreign language. In truth, millions of people of all types—rich and poor, scholars and manual laborers, old and young—already do it. Because most of us were not born to it, we find that it is something that has to be learned, and that takes time, patience and dedication. But we can all do it!

I quickly dismissed its glamour as too shallow an explanation of my drive. It was, I came to realize, something that I simply had to do. Something inside, my soul, was calling out for it. And I had little choice but to respond.

This self-analysis is necessary at this point to help you to put things into perspective. Take some time now to consider why you want to talk to your Celtic Angels.

The next thing you need to decide is what you want to say to your Celtic Angels. Do you have a particular question you want to ask? Is there a problem you want an answer to?

For the Druids and then the Celtic saints, the Celtic Angels were companions and helpers, advising and aiding where they could. The angels, however, did have their own agenda, with plans and schemes to be implemented. Whether or not they could see into the future is open to speculation. In my own experience there is nothing to suggest that they can see the future any more clearly than we can. They do seem to be more aware of events elsewhere than we are and so are able to say, for example, that you are going to get a telephone call or an interesting letter.

They cannot, or will not, give you the winning numbers in the national lottery. Celtic Angels are here primarily to help you on your spiritual journey. I well remember trying to argue that if they would just let me win enough money, I could build a great Celtic Heritage Centre. Think of all the good we could do, I used to argue. Think of the people we could introduce to the beliefs and values of the ancient Celts. All this to no avail. It took time and experience but I can see now that this would not have helped me to grow spiritually. Instead of finding the time I need to meditate, walk the hills and study, I would have been submerged in plans, strategies and accounts.

So sometimes the Celtic Angels seem to act in ways that may seem truculent or even obstreperous. But every question, every proposal, every plan they will judge in terms of whether or not it is in our own spiritual good. That can be a very hard measurement.

Imagine you have a friend who is going through a difficult period; perhaps their long-term relationship has broken up. You want to be there for them; to comfort, support and reassure them that there is a brighter future. You might appeal to your angels to help to support this person in their time of need. Your angels will judge that request in terms of how it will affect you. It may be that you need to work with your friend not just for their good but for yours as well. Maybe you have issues from an earlier relationship that have never been resolved: resentments that you have never put to rest or feelings of lack of self-worth that have never been totally expunged. Perhaps only by reliving these times with your friend can you move forward as well. In situations like that, your Celtic Angels might not only refuse to act, they might even make it worse by pointing out all these issues to you.

The relationship between the spirit world and the human world is still a mysterious one to us. The Celts knew that there were certain times when the veil between the worlds was at its thinnest. And at these times people could walk from one world to the other, sometimes without even intending to! The most powerful of these times was at Samhain: Halloween.

On a day-by-day basis, the most powerful time to try to reach the spirit realms is not midnight, as you might imagine, but rather at dusk. Dusk is a strange time when nothing is quite what it seems. As shadows lengthen, bushes and trees take on strange new outlines. Also you cannot define dusk. You have daylight and you have night. Dusk is the time in between, but one slowly fades into the other and this lack of clarity enchanted the Celts.

Walking at dusk is a most magical time. Gradually, so slowly that you cannot notice it, darkness falls. Sometimes it seems as if the blackness is dripping from the leaves of the trees and creeping around the boulders in the wall. It flows over the ground and laps your ankles. Who cannot fail to be moved at a time like that?

As the Celts counted from dark to light, dusk on the day after Halloween is the most powerful time of all. However you do not have to wait until then. To begin with you will find it easier to converse with your angels if you are outside in nature or at a sacred site at dusk. Once you have established contact and are comfortable with the exercises, then you can start working indoors and at times that suit you.

ANGEL MEDITATION

Find a space where you feel comfortable and will not be disturbed. Light a candle and say your invocation.

When you are ready, do the Celtic Meditation up to the point where you are floating in a warm, contented cloud of peace and relaxation. Inside you are glowing with white light.

Now imagine that white light beginning to change color. Slowly it becomes infused with a pale yellow until it becomes a golden white color. Now the energy is stirring inside and you sense a tingle of excitement. Feel the pressure build up inside you until you imagine you could burst. Channel all that pressure up through your head into a fountain of energy shooting skyward. As the golden white light races towards the heavens, you are not emptied inside, rather you are as full as ever.

This beacon will attract spirits and angels from all around. Now you need to show them that you are in control and totally aware of what you are doing.

Stop the energy flow and, instead of a fountain, imagine golden white globes emerging. As each globe, maybe twelve inches across, emerges, imagine it drifting up like a bubble until it is captured by a Celtic Angel. Quickly you will gather around a coterie of angels drifting maybe forty or fifty yards from you.

Hold that image in your mind. Now say aloud, "Greeting to all my Celtic Angels. I believe, however, that one is special to me; there is one who wishes to talk with me and help me on my spiritual journey. Please tell me your name."

You should get a reply almost immediately. You may hear a voice or, more commonly, a name will simply appear in your mind. If you do not, don't be alarmed. It may be that you are just unable to hear them clearly. Perhaps you have not tuned in to the spiritual dimensions as well as you think you have. It is an extremely difficult thing to do and to sustain. If this happens, wait and try again after a couple of days or so.

If you feel that you are connected but that the Celtic Angels are simply not replying, then it may be that they do not think you are ready for a personal relationship. And if that seems likely, carry on working with the angels in general and try again perhaps a month later.

In most cases, however, the reply is loud and instant. Intuitively I feel that the name you are given is something personal to you and your angel, and should not be shared.

Again, aloud, thank the Celtic Angels for their help. Close down the golden light and see it return within you to a white pure light. Wait for a couple of minutes and then, when you are ready, pull up your roots and then sense yourself return to the now.

Feel your body around you. Wait for a few more moments and then open your eyes. When you are ready, do your closing down ceremony.

Celtic Angels do not, of course, have names, this is simply for our convenience. There are no circumstances where we would form a close loving relationship with another person and not know their name.

Indeed names are so important that many people change them because they feel the name they were given as a child no longer reflects who they are. And so it is with the Celtic Angels. The name that you are given is something that should resonate with you for some reason. It may be the name of a deceased relative whom you felt particularly close to, or an inspiring figure from history or mythology who stands for attributes you value or aspire to.

In my own case the name was a character from the Arthurian legends. Like many people, I have, for as long as I can remember, been fascinated by the story of King Arthur. I have studied the histories of the time and found the quest for the historical Arthur fascinating. The character picked, however, had particular relevance for me at this point in my life. I knew nothing of him, though my partner remembered a couple of stories.

We sell Mind, Body, Spirit books at some health fairs. While I was doing these exercises, we were in Dublin setting up a book stall at a show there. As we were laying out the books on our stall, my partner picked out a book and said, "That's strange!" He was holding a book with the name of my Celtic Angel. We looked at each other. "Did you order this?" he asked. But he already knew the answer because he does all the ordering. Yet he had no memory of it.

The name my Celtic Angel had chosen obviously was designed to get me to think in a particular way; to see connections and draw some kind of conclusions. So it should be with you. After you have finished your meditation, get your Angel Journal and write down why you think that name was chosen and then consider what action is called for. It may be you will feel drawn to visit a particular sacred site; or research the meaning of the name. Like me, it may lead you into new, exciting areas of awareness and study. Whatever arises, consider it a gift, and a challenge!

The Angel Meditation is the normal method of seeking to communicate with your angels. As your relationship deepens and intensifies, they will be drawn more and more into the material world. Nonetheless this is always the way to start.

Opening up to Your Angels

Your Celtic Angels want you to succeed. They want you to advance spiritually, to learn the lessons that need to be learned, and live the experiences that need to be gone through. They are here for you. And together you will win.

But to do this you need to be totally honest with them. Not only will they know if you are not telling the whole story, you will know as well. Like working with a counselor or therapist, you will only progress if you keep nothing back. But unlike working with a professional, the relationship with your Celtic Angels is two-way. While the Celtic Angels have no secrets or worries to tell, they will discuss their thoughts and how they see issues that you describe.

TELLING A SECRET

This is a necessary first step for you. We all have secrets. From early childhood we learn that sometimes it is better to keep something to ourselves rather than share it with our parents or other children. As we grow up the practice becomes ingrained. Most secrets are fairly harmless. It might be that we don't really like some of our in-laws; or think the ties our boss wears are hideous. Some, however, are more profound, and often the more dangerous the secret, the more we hide it away. To tell anyone such a secret would demand a huge amount of trust from us. We have to believe that they will not reject us or betray our confidence. It is the sign of true friendship.

They say a problem shared is a problem halved and the same may be true of our innermost secrets. The more serious the secret, the more it can gnaw away at us as guilt and anger vie for our attention. And of course all the energy that takes up is time we could have been spending on more positive and life-enhancing events.

Do the Angel Meditation. Once you are surrounded by Celtic Angels, pause and simply float in that space, surrounded by all the angels. You may be able to see them in your mind's eye, or you may simply sense them flowing around you.

Call out for your special angel, using their name. You will feel them standing just behind you. They may touch you. One angel, who is not even my Anamcara, rests his hand on my shoulder. And from that a great calming strength flows through me. I sometimes find it makes it much easier to talk to him because of that.

Whisper out loud your secret. Do not expect any sharp intake of breath or shocked words. Expect silence, and your angel should simply thank you for sharing that with them. You have not invited any comment or help and they will offer none.

Celtic Angels often communicate using emotions or images and you may find that after having shared this experience with the Celtic Angel you feel a strong outburst of emotion. You may laugh or cry; feel exhilarated or relieved. This reaction is coming from your Celtic Angel working with you to make your life better. Take some time there with your angels before you start your closing down ceremony.

Depending on your life, this is an exercise that you may want to repeat several times. The more you open up to the Celtic Angel, the deeper and more meaningful your relationship will become.

Asking Questions and Understanding the Answers

As you work more and more with your angels, communication with them will become easier. Even so, sometimes it can be a difficult task to make them comprehend what you are asking and to understand the relevance of their reply. Often they will ignore your question altogether, answering the question they feel you should have asked.

I experienced a stark example of this. We were going to look at a house that was for sale nearby. I was quite excited as I have always wanted a house by the sea. That morning in my meditations I asked my Anamcara if the house would be suitable for us. His reply was that I should be thinking about my mother who was going into the hospital that day. While his reply bore no relationship to my question, it did direct me to where my priorities should lie. Suitably chastened, I thanked him for his answer.

However, thinking on this exchange later, I saw greater issues at work. I had effectively gotten sucked into material concerns when, as he pointed out, more important issues were at stake.

Problems that loom large in our lives, issues at work, troubles with the neighbors seem trivial or non-existent to our angels. They have little or no bearing on our spiritual development and so do not interest them. Just as they should be of little concern to us as well.

How you word questions is important. "Should I buy a new car?" is not the same as "Should I buy a new car from my friend?" That said, you are not in a court of law and the Celtic Angels will understand the intent behind the question. So while it is useful to work out exactly what you want to ask, do not worry too much about it.

Nonetheless, often the wisdom and considered advice of our Celtic Angels can be really helpful. If you have a problem you would like them to advise you on, try the following exercise.

DREAMING A PROBLEM AWAY WITH YOUR CELTIC ANGELS

Do this exercise at night, just as you are going to sleep. Although you may usually light a candle when you say your invocation, you may feel that it's not a good idea to leave a candle burning all night. In that case light some incense instead. Or, if you prefer, sprinkle a few drops of lavender water on your pillow, saying your invocation at the same time.

Now follow the instructions for the Angel Meditation. Feel the Celtic Angels all around you; call on your own Celtic Angel and feel their presence beside you.

Ask for their help in solving a problem, and explain why you need their help. You may wish to say that you've been worried about it for days and you find you can't meditate or even think about your angels because the problem is taking up so much energy.

Your angel should then ask you what the problem is. They may actually say the words, or you may simply sense that they are happy to listen to you.

After you have told them about the problem, you need to wait for the reply. This will come in your dreams.

In the morning, after you have written down your dreams, say your closing down ceremony. Take some time before trying to understand how the dreams answer your problem. On the face of it there may seem to be no connection, but there will be. You just have to find it.

Celtic Angels Are with You All the Time

Philip Pullman in the *His Dark Materials* trilogy created an alternative universe where people had visible talking dæmons (a spirit companion that was an integral part of a person's soul, not to be confused with "demon," which is an evil spirit) in the shape of an animal or bird connected to them by a psychic bond so that they could never be far apart. For children the companion dæmons would change shape as the mood and emotions of the child changed. As an adult, however, they became fixed into an external manifestation of the character of the person. Hence a sly, deceitful person might have a fox, while a happy, loving, trusting person might have a golden Labrador dog.

There would be a profound comfort in knowing that there was someone else there for you all the time. Someone who shares every moment and is totally, 100 percent on your side. Imagine having someone there with whom you can talk about all your worries and problems, discuss what actions to take and even share all the good times. Think how great it would be to have such a companion.

Well, in fact that is what your Celtic Angels are. Though instead of only one, you have a whole group of angels with you at all times. Try the following exercise to give you some feel of what that is like.

WALKING WITH THE CELTIC ANGELS

Find an open piece of ground. Preferably somewhere wild: a mountainside, empty beach or high pasture. Failing that, a park or playing field would do. Walk out until you have a wide space around you.

Now you need to do your opening ritual. Outdoors, candles are often not that practical. So you need to have planned an alternative ceremony. An action of some kind is appropriate. One option that appeals to me is to scatter some scented potpourri as you walk. Another idea is to pour a little water from a bottle as a libation to the gods of any site.

Next, do the Angel Meditation. Once the Celtic Angels have gathered, stand still for several minutes and sense them all around you. Slowly become aware again of the noises of everyday life. Little by little let your awareness return to where you are standing, while at the same time still sensing the Celtic Angels whirling around you. This is not easy to do and it may take you many attempts to achieve this mixture of sensations.

Moving on to the next stage, prepare to open your eyes. As you focus on the surroundings, keep the sensations of the Celtic Angels all around you. This is actually not as difficult as you might imagine. We already use non-standard senses to tell us, for example, when someone is standing close behind us or if someone across a room is staring at us. We are using these same senses now to appreciate the movements of the Celtic Angels. So while you may not see the angels, you will nonetheless be aware of them.

Take your angels for a walk. Sense them sweeping and swirling around you as you stroll along. Pay particular attention to the sensations that the angels evoke in you. Find somewhere comfortable and sit down. Perhaps under an ash tree.

When you are ready, close your eyes and thank the Celtic Angels for their company. Then start your closing-down ceremony. When you are finished, take a few minutes to come around.

In truth, the Celtic Angels are with us all the time. Wherever we are, so are they. It is just that until now we have not been aware of them.

Try to remember the sensations you experienced as the angels flowed around you. Over the next few days whenever you are out walking in the countryside, in a park or any large open space, try to sense the angels around you. When you do feel their presence, you will realize what a huge comfort it is. And once it becomes second nature to you, it will be possible for you to conjure up the angels at any time: in the house; at stressful meetings; sitting in the car. And it feels so good to know that there are other people rooting for you. And don't forget, you and your Celtic Angels make a winning team. Together you are invincible!

NINE

Face to Face with Your Celtic Angel: A Personal Relationship

Talking with your Celtic Angels is a powerful spiritual experience. It opens you up to a whole set of new emotions. You are no longer alone and the more you converse with them, the stronger and more meaningful the link between you and the spiritual realms will become.

As you are aware from Part One of *Anam Cara Wisdom*, there is a huge controversy over whether angels can or cannot materialize in our world. This despite thousands, if not millions, of stories of how angels have intervened in people's lives to save them from imminent danger. One story from Amsterdam that has always stayed with me was of a woman whose child had wandered out onto the road. As she ran out to get him, a man appeared from nowhere, swept the child into his arms and carried the boy back onto the pavement. The relieved woman grabbed the child and then turned to thank the man, but there was no one there although she could see quite clearly up and down the street.

Even in our ordinary day-to-day life there are occasions when the angels intervene. One of my friends tells of the time she stepped out into a road and never saw a car racing toward her. Literally at the last possible second she felt herself being yanked back, to the extent that she almost lost her footing. Not immediately realizing the danger she had been in, she turned to berate the person behind her. But there was no one there.

Celtic Angels most definitely do materialize in our world. They appear as solid beings capable of touching us, eating and drinking our food, even making tools and laboring beside us. In the traditional Breton tale of the unhappy shepherdess Yvonne, she meets and then marries a shining man, a term normally reserved for an angel. In this case one that walks in the real world.

In this chapter we are going to take our relationship with our Celtic Angels to a new level by not only talking with them, but actually seeing them. First of all we will do this in our mind's eye and then, when we are ready, actually in the flesh. One of the most fantastic experiences possible is to walk through the woods with your Celtic Angels at your side. The sense of calm, peace and interconnectedness almost overpowers you and leaves you feeling strangely calm and loved.

In Your Mind's Eye

As we have said before, we are surrounded by Celtic Angels all the time. These anonymous angels are attracted by our spiritual energy and seek to accompany us in our life experiences. They can also be very helpful in everyday aspects of life and many of the Angel Whispers you hear may well originate with them rather than with the Celtic Angels closest to us.

Already, when you meditate, you may see them. Perhaps not clearly, but you may see some sort of outline or shape.

In this section we are concerned with the Celtic Angels who are closest to you. These are Celtic Angels who are not anonymous, but have personalities and with whom you have already been conversing. For many people there is only one; others have several. In the main, I only have one, though there is another Celtic Angel who guards a site I visit and I will often sit with him.

It may be that, like me, you are old enough to remember televisions when you had to tune in to the channel manually, much as you still have to do with non-digital radio. To begin with the picture would be hazy and although you knew there was something there, you couldn't see what. Gradually, by fine-tuning the picture, it would become clear. Over a period of time you would then learn how to switch channels by turning the knob just the right amount to go from one clear channel to the next.

Trying to see your Celtic Angels is very much like that. To begin with you might find that you only get glimpses or faint images that fade away as soon as you look directly at them. In due course, as with the television, you will be able to switch from one world to another relatively easily. It is, however, important that you are patient and tolerant as you work on this exercise. This is not something that will happen overnight. It takes months and months of practice but, at the end of it all, you will achieve a most amazing result: the ability to talk with and see your personal Celtic Angels.

Preparing to See Your Celtic Angels

There are some tools we can use to empower our own abilities. The first is an Angel Altar. If you have not already done so, this is the time to create one (see p. 74). An altar acts as a focus for you while you meditate and certainly my Anamcara prefers, when I am at home, that I use my own Angel Altar.

Next you need to prepare yourself for this most sacred of tasks. The more you do this exercise and succeed the less preparation you need to undertake. Even so, I am still surprised how, sometimes, things seem much easier after careful preparation.

First of all plan this event well in advance. Give yourself several days to prepare. Try to surround yourself with little angel mementoes to remind you that the Celtic Angels are all around. Try to imagine what it will be like finally to see them. Ask yourself, Am I ready? All this is to help you to focus on what you are going to do. Read through this exercise several times so that you are familiar with it. Feel a gentle sense of anticipation surround you. What will your angel look like?

On the day in question, make sure that you are at peace and not preoccupied with anything. Spend some time just sitting quietly, thinking of nothing special. Relax, sit and read a novel or go for a walk in the garden or countryside. Generally have a lazy, tranquil time.

An hour or so before dusk or whatever time you have chosen to do the exercise, take a shower or bath to cleanse yourself. Use no soap or scents, just the clear calm water itself. This is an ancient ritual based on beliefs in the healing and spiritual properties of water. Try to feel the cleansing power of the water on your skin. Imagine the clutter and debris of day-to-day life flowing away, leaving you fresh and renewed.

Dress wearing only natural materials. Wear plain un-dyed cotton if possible. This is to help maintain the pure natural feeling that you are trying to create and to ensure that nothing interferes with the spiritual energy that you emit.

Next, sit quietly for a few minutes and calm your mind. If you are outside you can try to switch your awareness away from yourself so that you notice the birds singing, the rustling of the breeze in the trees and the distant noises of the land around you. You might even feel the skirl of the Celtic Angels.

Only now, when you are relaxed and at peace, are you ready to proceed. It is now time to go and meet your Celtic Angel.

MEETING YOUR CELTIC ANGEL

When you are ready light the three candles on your altar and sit facing them. Say your invocation. Light your incense. Focus on each of the elements on your altar. Think of the beauty of nature, the inspiration of the incense blowing on the air, the cool calmness of the water, the power of fire and the productive serenity of the earth. And as you enter this world, you make it complete.

Close your eyes. Do the Angel Meditation and when you are surrounded by all the Celtic Angels and the golden white bubbles are floating around you, stop and relax. Enjoy the moment for what it is.

When you are ready say out loud, "I would like to meet my personal Celtic Angel." Add the name of the angel you were given previously. Slowly repeat this. As you do so, ask yourself how this feels. Does it feel good and a natural progression from where you are? Assuming that it does, then you can move on to the next stage. If for any reason it does not feel right, then simply thank the Celtic Angels for their love and support, be content, wait for a few minutes and then make your closing down ceremony.

Notice how the image of the golden bubbles and the Celtic Angels is fading out. You are floating now in a warm, safe place. Repeat your request to yourself and watch as a new landscape begins to emerge into view.

You are in a high meadow. Away in the distance where the land begins to slope down, you can see tall, dark green trees, but here, in the middle, there is just short grass. In the center of your vision you can see a table and two chairs. It might be a park picnic set, or a bistro café table. It doesn't matter. Someone is sitting facing you as you approach. It is your personal Celtic Angel.

You already know the name of your personal Celtic Angel. So greet them and ask them if that is their name. They will probably invite you to sit with them. Sit down facing them. What happens next will vary from person to person. However, it will be very simple and very beautiful.

The first time I met the angel who went on to become my Anamcara, we simply sat facing each other. He took my hand, as he always does. He is about my age but with a Scandinavian look. His face is perhaps broader than most but he has a constant smile which lights up his whole being and seems to radiate out from him, rather like a Cheshire cat.

He is almost always calm, serene and thoughtful. Sometimes, though, when he is caught up in something, he can be quite animated and I have even seen him punch the air in a quite un-angel kind of way after we had achieved something really special.

Remember that your angel could appear to you in any form but they will choose a form that is comfortable for you and non-threatening. And once they have appeared to you in a particular way, they will not change it.

With my Anamcara, we rarely do more than sit and discuss whatever issues are prevalent at that time. Occasionally he will suggest that we walk and when that happens, he takes my arm and we stroll across the wide open meadow of grass. Your experiences may be similar, or you may find that they take you to other sacred sites, or let you see things that are happening elsewhere. Each relationship is unique.

When you are ready to close, or when your Celtic Angel indicates it is time to go, bow slightly and thank them for their time. Now simply pull back, like a film camera, from the scene. You can, if you prefer, get up and walk away but if you do this you should walk backwards, always facing your Celtic Angel.

Now slowly become aware of sitting, once again, in front of your altar. Take a few minutes to reacquaint yourself with where you are and then blow out the candles. Make your closing-down gesture. Write down all that happened in your Angel Journal and then take ten minutes or so to relax and come around.

When Your Celtic Angel Appears in the Flesh

As well as in your mind's eye, Celtic Angels will appear to you in the flesh. They look just like us. Remember angels, even in the Bible, almost never appeared wearing wings. One Celtic Angel I meet from time to time doesn't even like being called an angel. When I asked him how I should describe him, however, he couldn't offer any other appropriate word.

While you can meet and work with your Celtic Angels any time in your mind's eye, it is up to them if and when they appear to you in the flesh. You cannot force your angel to appear, nor should you seek to summon them. It is clear that while many people experience short and sudden visitations, far fewer people experience long-term encounters.

In Celtic sagas and hagiographies, the Celtic Angels only appeared for long periods of time to those men and women who had dedicated their life to following spiritual pursuits. In other words, if you want your Celtic Angels to appear regularly, then you need to create the right ambience for that to happen. The more you immerse yourself in your spiritual pursuits, the more likely it is that your angels will appear.

This has certainly been my experience. The times when it has happened have not been the most dramatic in my life nor was the message imparted of such profound importance that it demanded an appearance. These visitations, however, because they are rare, become ever more precious. I can recall every aspect of every visit and treasure the emotions and love that the visits engendered.

St. Mungo's Church at Mungrisdale, in the Cumbrian Lake District, is a remarkably unremarkable church. Clearly of great antiquity, the site is nonetheless devoid of any of the usual signs of a sacred site. To a great extent, it just looks as if the churchyard is part of a field. This is however a remarkable place. It lies at the entrance to a short valley in front of an amazing dumpy hill, a hill that has the exact shape of a cream pastry. Tracks lead from here up to Saddleback or Blencathra, where legend states King Arthur and his knights lie sleeping. It is tempting to see the church as the gatekeeper to this magical place.

It was here that my Anamcara danced around the inside of the church. For me there was no great sense of spirituality about it. But he loved it. It was peaceful and calm and a pleasant place to sit and meditate but there was no great presence, at least for me. And yet that sense of place has remained. It is an inner calm that I have taken from there, without even being aware of doing it. As well as the pleasure of seeing my Anamcara splendidly happy!

Celtic Angels Prefer Nature

Where and when are two important factors in increasing the likelihood of you meeting your Celtic Angels in the flesh. Celtic Angels much prefer the energies of the natural world to those that surround us indoors. In Celtic mythology the magical world appeared outside the castle or the village; Druids lived in small camps in the woods; all religious services and work with the magical and spiritual forces occurred in the sacred groves, rocky pinnacles or beside the restless sea. Merlin, the great Druid of Arthurian legend, lived in a cave and spent much of his life wandering in the hills and forests of south Wales.

Celtic saints also prayed out of doors. Often they would meditate for days sitting on a broad rock, in the mouth of caves or on mountain tops. And it would be to those sites that the Celtic Angels would come. St. Cuthbert when he retreated from Lindisfarne went to the island of Farne. There the Celtic Angels came and helped him to build a cell for himself. They carried wood from the mainland and, according to some legends, even brought food to sustain him on these bleak islands.

The more natural the land, the more untouched by human hands, the more spiritual it is. As you seek to work with the Celtic Angels more and more, so you should feel the call of the wild. You may suddenly, during a meditation, think of a sacred site or a beach you haven't visited in a while.

Treat these Angel Whispers as summonses. They need not be obeyed immediately but try to visit them in the near future. If you do not manage this, do not despair. It is simply a missed opportunity, nothing more. Your angels will try another time and in another way.

As you are tuning in to the energies of the Celtic Angels, you will find that there are some unexpected consequences. One is that in your home you may find your tastes changing. Do not be surprised if you find yourself using more natural fabrics; opening windows and doors more; buying more plants and spending longer tending them; becoming more suspicious of radio waves. These changes are to be celebrated because they are influenced by the same energies that are pulling you and your Celtic Angels together.

Time of Day

Time of day, and indeed of year, can also be very important in your work with the Celtic Angels. The Celts discovered that some times of the day and periods of the year were more powerful than others in helping them to work with the spirit worlds. And this is also true of angel work. Certainly over Samhain (Halloween) you should try to be outside and on your own as much as possible. Dusk and, to a lesser extent, dawn are important times.

The full moon is another powerful point when the land energies seem to be stronger and so the Celtic Angels find it easier to appear. At the full moon I go out for walks in the countryside, trying to be aware of the moon as much as possible and appreciating how remarkable and beautiful it is. As I stroll down narrow country lanes or follow tracks through groves of trees with the moon sending dappled white light all around me, that is a time when I often feel closest to the Celtic Angels. I feel them dance around me and then I sense my Anamcara walking beside me, just a step behind.

Committing to Your Celtic Angels

When your Celtic Angels appear, it is because you have made it possible. In fact you are the most important factor. If you are busy rushing from here to there, always surrounded by people and with a mind filled with a dozen worries, then this is not conducive to your Celtic Angels. In fact, if they did appear, you might not even notice. At night I often walk my dog past a fairy dell. Some days you can really feel the presence of these beings, and there's a magic in the atmosphere so that the very air seems to glitter. I love that. Other times, I'm so preoccupied that I've walked the dog past the dell twice and not noticed anything.

So you need to begin following a spiritual practice. This does not mean that you have to renounce all your worldly possessions and family and go and live in a cave in the middle of the desert, unless you want to. What it means is accepting that you want to be a more spiritual person: more aware, more compassionate and, most importantly, more conscious of the spiritual energies that are all around you.

To a large extent this book is intended as a guide for you in this acceptance. As you walk with the angels or do an Angel Meditation, then you are becoming more spiritual. And you should find that spiritual practice is very rewarding; the more you do, the more you want to do. You are particularly lucky because the Celtic Angels want you to succeed and so will try to help you every step of the way.

What follows are suggestions on how to make your life more spiritual and so enhance your links with your Celtic Angels. Initially you should follow this list, but listen to your intuition and adapt, change and add exercises to develop your own unique program.

1. Good morning, Angels! Light a candle first thing in the morning and spend a few minutes sitting quietly with it. Think of your angels and lessons they have taught you. You might want to read an Angel Affirmation or draw an Angel Card and contemplate the message your angels have given you for the day. You can make your own sets by choosing uplifting words or phrases and writing them on pieces of paper. If you prefer, nowadays there are several attractive sets you can buy.

2. Wear or carry something to remind you of your angels, and make a point, several times a day, of touching the brooch or lapel pin and reminding yourself of your angels and their love for you.

Try to have something at work too. It need not be overtly angelic. One idea is to buy an attractive small flowering plant. Sit it on your altar for a few days while you meditate and then take it into work with you. Then every time you look at it, you will be reminded of the Celtic Angels.

3. Choose one kind of incense and use it all the time on your Angel Altar. After a while you will associate that scent with meditating and communing with your angels. Burn it at other times as well, and this will give you a regular reminder to keep your Celtic Angels foremost in your mind.

4. Find time to meditate every day. Set aside a period to be on your own and do the Celtic Meditation, outlined in Chapter 7. It only takes about half an hour. But this time must be very precious to you and you need to commit to it. Not only are you doing this for yourself, you are also affirming to the Celtic Angels that they are important to you.

5. Do a good deed every day on behalf of your angels. It could be giving money to charity, helping a friend in need or just paying attention to the plight of others that you read about in the newspapers or hear about in the news. When you do an action in the name of your Celtic Angels, you create a link which they will use to magnify your gift in a thousand precious ways.

There are many other actions you can take. This list hopefully gives you some ideas. You need to look at how you spend your money, what you eat, what you work at and many more issues. But it can sometimes be daunting to see so much in a list. Better to get started and as you begin to change your life and your habits, other issues will naturally arise and you can make further changes as you feel appropriate.

The Appearance of Celtic Angels

Somehow, after all this, you would imagine that when your Celtic Angels appear in the flesh it would be with great ceremony and fanfare. In fact that has not been my experience.

The first time it happened to me, I had been meditating with some silver birches at dusk on the day after Halloween. I had then started to gather some old dried birch wood for a fire and he just appeared!

Another time I was sitting by a burn listening to the sounds of the water, feeling my thoughts and worries flow out of me as the water burbled past. Then there he was standing beside me.

Remember that they will appear as you have seen them in your mind's eye. Don't forget that there is more than one Celtic Angel working with you and so you may see them in the flesh as well. This usually happens because they have some experience or knowledge that you need to hear. When a Celtic Angel appears to you in the flesh you should bow and greet them. If you know their name you should use it. Normally they will come straight to the point and tell you what they want you to know. Occasionally they will take more of an interest in the surroundings and maybe ask you some questions about your garden or the piece of ground they are standing in.

In my experience Celtic Angels neither fade away or suddenly disappear. Rather you seem to come to, as if out of a trance. And they are gone.

Be aware also that the Celtic Angels might not come to you in human form. Celtic gods and goddesses will often take the form of animals. Cernunnos, Lord of the Forest, King of the Animals would often appear as a stag running free in the forest. So it is with the Celtic Angels. St. Patrick, as he fought his doubts and uncertainties on the top of Croagh Patrick, was uplifted and strengthened when a crowd of angels appeared to him in the form of a flock of white birds that seemed to fill the sky with their brightness and energy.

So be conscious in your daily life that your angels may well be there to support and love you. Perhaps in a difficult meeting at work a white dove will come and sit on the window ledge; if you are having a hard time at home with the children, a white rabbit may appear on the back lawn. Whatever the creature, you will know intuitively that it is a Celtic Angel and its appearance will immediately help you to feel better and perhaps help to put events into perspective.

Celtic Angels surround you all the time. They are there for you. Sometimes of course it is nice for us to be reassured by actually seeing them with our own eyes. They know this. In fact, they do appear more than we realize. How do you know that the stranger who helped you when the car broke down, the woman who suddenly appeared in a deserted street to give you directions, the dog at the bus stop that allowed itself to be petted when you were upset, how do you know that these were not Celtic Angels?

Simply be aware. Once you look for signs that the Celtic Angels are all around you, you will be stunned at how often you really do spot them! And remember that Celtic tradition states that you should treat every stranger with courtesy and compassion because you don't know who, or what, they are.

TEN

Having an Anamcara

It was rare for an ancient Celt ever to be alone. In their villages they lived in fairly primitive houses with many people sharing one room and indeed one bed. Each village, or clachan, would be composed of perhaps up to a dozen houses. The men would fish, hunt or till the land, and the women would help with the farming as well as running the household. In each case they would be aided by other adults in the family.

With people, of course, would come chat and gossip and noise. Voices and the sounds of work filled your mind and prevented your soul from soaring free into the clear blue sky. Even today that can be true. In the Lake District in northwest England, there is a hill called after the fairies. Elva Hill lies to the northwest of Bassenthwaite Lake and, despite the teeming summer rain, I was determined to climb it and also visit the stunted stone circle on the side of the hill. As I stood on the top, with breathtaking views south across the narrow blue water squeezed between the dark murky mountains, I felt an echo of the magic that must have led the Norse men to name this hill after the elves. However, as I meditated and felt myself open up, I became aware, even there, of the sounds of traffic from the busy roads to the south and east of the hill.

It is only when you find total silence that you become aware of how much noise we surround ourselves with. Stop for a moment and listen. What do you hear? Noise is all around.

For most of us, the option of escaping to a mountain top in the Highlands is not possible on a day-by-day basis and so we can either get annoyed at the lack of peace or simply accept it. And after all you are never really alone; your Celtic Angels are always there with you.

For the ancient Celts, both druidic and Christian, family was very important. You were born and raised in an extended household. Not only would you have more brothers and sisters than most families have today, but most of the people who lived in your clachan would also be family: aunts and uncles; cousins and nieces and nephews. For the family was the basic building block of Celtic society.

To break away from your family was almost impossible. Even the druidic camps and later the Celtic monasteries were organized along family lines. Reinforcing the family was the practice, common among Celtic chiefs, of fostering out children to other households and receiving other children in return. This meant that children grew up with people who were not their parents but helped them to develop strong relationships with these other members of their wider family.

It is easy to see then how the role of the Anamcara would develop. Children would need someone they could trust, who would be on their side and to whom they could turn for help. Add on to this the role of tutoring, or at least overseeing the tutoring, and you have the basis of what an Anamcara is. Equally, there was very little opportunity for people to have real secrets and so the idea of confiding in another person would not be as traumatic as it can be for us today.

The Historical Anamcara

When you entered the Druid camp as a young boy or girl, there would be a period of settling in. You would then be appointed your first Anamcara. This would be an older Druid who would teach you the basics of Druidism. The Druid would almost certainly have several students with him and to begin with you would be little better than a servant. Gradually however, as you grew older, you would begin to learn skills and become more of an apprentice. As the years passed you would become an equal, perhaps even surpass the master, and the nature of the Anamcara relationship would have changed to one of equals. Eventually it would be time to move on and to start having pupils of your own. At that point your Anamcara might change as well, depending on what you both felt was for the best.

The Celtic saints maintained this system and developed it. Especially in the larger monasteries most of the teaching duties were assigned to specific monks. For the novice and whatever monk was assigned as the Anamcara, the relationship would be more one of companionship and shared experience than master and student.

All monks and nuns had an Anamcara, equal or more spiritually advanced than they were. For as St. Comgall of Bangor, one of the great Irish saints who died in A.D. 603, said, "A person without a soul friend is a body without a head." In many monasteries the two monks or nuns, acting as Anamchairde to each other, would share a cell and spend most of their time together. One writer compared them to a husband and wife team, though of course without the sex.

From the very beginning novices were instructed to hold nothing back when they were working with their Anamcara. There were to be no secrets, no half-truths or carefully constructed explanations. For the relationship to work you had to trust your Anamcara completely. This is actually not so difficult for young children, especially when there is no element of punishment or condemnation no matter what is said. This idea of trust may seem strange but I well remember my first civil service office job. The woman who sat near me was senior to me but very friendly and I confided in her that I had only taken the job because nothing else had been available and that I was still looking. I was horrified when she reported this to my boss. I had trusted her, believing I could rely on her. I still remember the dismay of realizing that I could trust no one in that office. Perhaps by nature we want to trust people. I hope so.

The Anamcara Today

In the modern world, you may already have experienced some kinds of Anamcara. Although the intense life-long spiritual coupling may be alien to us now, we all quest after it, albeit in other forms.

Some people have compared the Anamcara relationship to that of a priest in the confessional. And there is an element of that except that the Anamcara partner, even a senior monk, would not give absolution for sins. A better modern-day equivalent would be a counselor or therapist where you reveal all your innermost secrets in a private and confidential environment.

A long-term relationship like this might seem stifling to us. Most of us nowadays are brought up to be individuals with our own wishes and desires. We are quite distinct from everyone around us, even our partners and children.

The Anamcara relationship is in fact very liberating. The truth is that we spend a lot of time and energy living up to other people's expectations of us. In most cases we are 90 percent of what people think we are, but there is always that little bit that longs to be different: to go on a walk around the world or to take drugs and be out clubbing all night instead of attending the local city council meeting.

With our Anamcara we are 100 percent what we seem to be. There are no secrets. Desires would be spoken of and discussed, perhaps even acted on. Likes and dislikes would be assessed and understood. The whole process is incredibly invigorating.

Opening up to others is difficult. There are however occasions in the modern world when we do. The first is a kind of relationship with what we might consider a professional Anamcara. This is a short-term therapeutic association which generally we pay for. Here the professional has experience and knowledge that we wish to access. In order for us, as the client, to gain from this, we need to be totally honest. The first time I became aware of this was when I went for homeopathic treatment. We spent an hour and a half talking about me. It revealed to me how many half-lies we tell about ourselves. It is as if we create a whole history that is sort of true but with embellishments and the less pleasant aspects glossed over.

A second form of Anamcara is what we might call the informal Anamcara. This is the "best friend," someone we are very close to and share almost all our secrets with. It would be highly unusual for us to be totally honest, but best friends are nonetheless people we trust, who are there for us and to whom we can turn for help and advice.

A more obvious Anamcara relationship might be one that you have with your local spiritual leaders: church ministers, rabbis or mullahs. Again, like a best friend, they are there for us but, no matter how willing or friendly they are, we are only one of many people who have calls on their time. And even if we do call them a friend, there is still something of a professional relationship about the whole situation. Nonetheless they can help, especially when we have questions about spiritual matters.

Of course these spiritual leaders need not be formally linked to any religious institution. Sometimes we are simply drawn to people who have studied different aspects of spirituality. I have met many learned men and women whom I grew to respect and appreciate, yet they had no formal qualifications or role. For the spiritual traveler these people are so important. They are refreshing and inspiring; they can provide knowledge and experience that are crucial to us or they may simply reawaken within ourselves the realization that we want to find out more.

When you walk the spiritual path, these meetings happen all the time. One of the more bizarre examples of this was when I met a student of Zoroastrianism. I had been studying Gnostic Christianity and had been working backwards in time. I had just started to read a book about this religion, once so popular in northern Persia, but nowadays confined to one small area. And here, in a sauna in Edinburgh, I met an actual follower of the religion from that part of the world. Talking to this man helped me to understand a lot more about the emotion of the religion and even to see how it related to me and my own spiritual journey.

So, as can be seen, the essence of the idea of the Anamcara still exists with us today. More than that, many of us still crave its comfort and support. We recognize that to walk the spiritual path can be lonely and confusing. To have a friend and guide there with us may be just what we need.

Why Do We Need a Soul Friend?

Unlike the ancient Celts, today we are used to being on our own, at least in the Western world. From an early age most of us have our own bedrooms, or aspire to do so. We are no longer prepared to dedicate our lives to our families and to do whatever is deemed best for the future of the family. We have our own wishes and desires. We want to decide on the career we intend to pursue, how we want to lead our lives and what values and aspirations we wish to hold.

This individualism attends our spiritual development as well. While many people still regularly attend church, mosque, synagogue or chapel, most are no longer prepared to accept the word of the preacher without question. How many Catholics use birth control, or Jews cook on the Sabbath?

The dramatic fall in attendance at church, in all its forms, is not however marked with an equally sharp fall in people who believe that there is some kind of spiritual aspect to life. People are simply questioning the establishments of the major religions. And these organizations are finding it hard to respond.

However, we cannot simply float like flotsam on the spiritual sea; we do need some direction. A Church of Scotland minister once described to me the New Age as an era of mix-and-match religion, where you take the parts you like and reject the rest. He was of course ignoring the early history of the Christian Church, which did exactly this as well. However, he did have a point. We do need to accept that if we have no direction, no overall view, then all we can hope for is some pleasant, inspiring experiences and a degree of contentment. Which, of course, is no bad thing.

We need an Anamcara to help to give us that perspective and direction. By discussing our experiences and understandings, we can relate them to the bigger picture. In a very small way, I see this as I tour the country giving talks and workshops. Often after I have been talking about something, for example, that Celtic Angels are all around us and how we can experience that for ourselves, someone will come up to me and say, "You know I had that sensation, but I didn't know what it meant." One woman I remember talked about how she had always been drawn to a particular tree and loved to sit there.

She said to me that she used to have a feeling that she was not alone and it did not frighten her, it comforted her. She would tell the tree her secrets and it made her feel better. If she had been able to discuss all this with an Anamcara then she would have grasped the true significance of what she was feeling.

An Anamcara can also teach us. Anyone who is more experienced than we are has lessons to offer us. It may not stop us making mistakes, but it will help us to understand that it is a mistake and how to rectify it. Sadly, I have never found anyone like that and so have had to stumble on my way. There was one woman I met, Margaret, who died a few years ago. Even for the short time I knew her, I recognized in her someone who could teach me so much, and it is one of my regrets that we never managed to develop the relationship. However, I still remember her fondly and now only wish I had known how short a time we were destined to have together.

Finally, an Anamcara helps us to put everything into perspective. We must never forget that we are not exclusively spiritual creatures. We are possibly unique in that we link the upper spiritual worlds with the baser material ones. All our spiritual work must not overshadow our material needs. And those needs are not just food and water. We need to relax, to enjoy ourselves. Humankind are naturally gregarious and we need to acknowledge that. Even the most austere Celtic monasteries would celebrate when guests came to stay or it was a holy day. The monks may have fasted on Wednesdays and Fridays but not when they were entertaining, or being entertained.

There is always a danger of getting so wrapped up in your spiritual needs and wants that you forget the other needs in your life. One person I know discovered Buddhism and went through a period where all he wanted to do was to meditate, read, study and use his free time spiritually. His partner become increasingly frustrated at this and eventually an ultimatum was delivered. An Anamcara would have pointed out the need to tend his relationship long before it became a problem.

Preparing to Work with Your Anamcara

Finally in this chapter we want to look at the steps you need to take to get ready for working with your Anamcara. For most of us there is little opportunity for us to find someone who encompasses all the attributes that we would want in our Anamcara. We are therefore fortunate that we can turn to our Celtic Angels. Whether your Anamcara is human or angelic, there are still some issues that we need to deal with.

FREEING OUR SOUL

Our relationship with our Anamcara is not just person to person, but soul to soul. For the relationship to work, therefore, we need to open up to our soul and free it.

You can think of your soul as a small flame dancing in your heart. This is an image common to many religions around the world. Take a moment now to visualize this flame. In your mind's eye, see yourself as a clear glass body. Within it see the pinkness of your heart. See your soul flame flickering there.

For the soul to be free, we have to bypass the "me." We have to forget all our wants and desires. Instead we have to concentrate on that little flame fluttering in our heart.

Take some time now to think of that flame. Find a place where you feel comfortable and will not be disturbed. When you are ready, light a candle and say your invocation. Now do the Celtic Meditation.

When you are floating, pause there to enjoy the sensation. See yourself as a glass body filled with white light. Focus and see your heart beating and within it the small solitary flame of your soul. In your mind send it waves of love. Tell it you love it, want to care for it and see it flourish.

Do you feel anything in return? Does the flame change at all?

Now stop. And rest, floating in the inky red darkness, safe and serene. Think of a truly wonderful moment in your life when you felt totally loved and loved in return. Perhaps it was when you got married, or maybe just an occasion sharing something special with friends. Try to remember how you felt and once more send waves of love to your soul flame. Again, see if you feel any response.

And rest.

For a final time, feel the full force of love that you can muster and send it to the flame flickering in your heart.

This time feel yourself flow around your glass body and sense the whole image change as your soul flame leads you on a journey. Feel a sense of traveling, of distance and then see where you end up.

Your soul flame may be sharing an important event from your past. It may be showing you something that it wants you to do or it may be simply sharing something inspiring with you.

When you are ready to return home, thank your soul flame for sharing that experience with you. And then, in the darkness, feel yourself coming back into your own body. After a couple of minutes, open your eyes and sit quietly until you feel ready to move.

This exercise helps you to understand a little of the needs and desires of your soul. It also helps you to appreciate that we are all three parts in one: a mind, everything that is "me"; a body, the machine that we inhabit; and a spirit, the sacred flame that connects us with the divine.

Creating an Intimate Relationship

For most of us today we are simply not used to being so open with anyone else. Even within long-term relationships such as marriage, we tend to hold back a little of what is us. We spend time apart pursuing different hobbies or interests.

It is true that there may be times in our lives when we do turn to another for support and help. You might turn to your local minister or priest in times of bereavement or other traumatic experiences.

So much trust is involved in this relationship. You have to be able to trust that the person is knowledgeable in matters spiritual; that they are not going to take advantage of you; that their thinking on matters resonates with you and that you feel able to trust their judgement. But at some point you will have to learn to be totally open with them. Try this next exercise now and when it is finished imagine how you would feel reading this to your Anamcara.

OPENING UP

Find somewhere quiet to sit. Although this is not a spiritual exercise, you nonetheless want somewhere you feel safe and secure, where you will not be interrupted or overheard. Now open your Angel Journal. Light a candle and say your invocation. Take a separate page in your journal and head it, "Ten Secrets I Have Never Told Anyone."

I suspect you are already feeling nervous and apprehensive at the idea of committing such things to your journal. If you prefer, take a large fire-proof plate and place your lit candle in the middle of it. Now take a loose sheet of paper and cut it into ten fair-sized pieces. Take one piece and write your first secret on it.

Look at what you have written. Think how it came about. Try to imagine people's reaction if you were to tell them. Depending on the secret you might smile and realize that most people either might have guessed or wouldn't really care. Even if they were shocked, true friends would rally around you.

When you are ready, say it out loud. You'll be surprised at how difficult that is. You might want to say it several times until you feel at least a little more comfortable saying it. Then, when you are ready, burn it.

Of course you might not think that you have ten secrets, or that the only ones you can think of are so minor that they are of no consequence. Not everyone has a secret lover or a dead body buried in the garden. But we all do have many secrets we don't want anyone else to know about: secret thoughts about our family; dubious financial dealings when we were young; addictions or secret desires. However, if you cannot think of ten secrets, delay this exercise for a week and meanwhile think about your hidden secrets whenever you get a chance. When you realize one, write it down in your journal. Of course it doesn't have to be exactly ten; nine, eight or fifteen would do!

When you have finished writing down your secrets and contemplating them, close your Angel Journal. You may well feel what you have written burning away in your journal, but that sensation will lessen.

Now sit for a few minutes. You may well feel different now, perhaps lighter, unburdened in some way. That is good. Smile, you are happy.

When you are ready, do your closing ceremony.

When you are working with your Anamcara these secrets are the sort of thing you will have to confide to them. You have to be totally open with them and that is difficult.

In the times of the Celtic saints, Anamcara were probably appointed by the monastery leaders, at least initially. It was possible to change Anamcara as you grew up and moved on to new monasteries or to do missionary work abroad. Some saints, such as St. Aeddan of Ferns in County Wexford in Ireland, had a Celtic Angel to nominate an Anamcara. St. David found himself in close proximity to a great holy man, St. Justinan from Brittany, and the two great men agreed to become Anamchairde for each other. Indeed even today their bones lie together in St. David's Cathedral.

For us today, unless we are very fortunate, it is highly unlikely that we will meet someone who can fulfill all the characteristics of a good Anamcara. As we have already said, we can get around this problem by following the example of the great Celtic saints and having an angel as our Anamcara. How we do this will be discussed in the next chapter.

ELEVEN

Your Celtic Angel as Anamcara

Together we have traveled far along the path that winds through the woods. You have become aware of the spiritual realms that surround us. You can feel the Celtic Angels as they whirl around and you have even talked to them and seen your personal angels. Now, however, is the most dramatic step of all. Now you are going to commit yourself to an angel who will become your Anamcara—your soul friend.

From now on you will never be alone. From now on an angel will always be at your side, holding your hand and leading you towards spiritual fulfillment. Celtic Angels are gentle, loving masters. They demand little and give so much. They will help you to find your purpose in life and then help you to lead the life you were born to live.

Asking Your Angel

Your personal angel has already come forward and met you. However, you cannot just assume that they will want to be your Anamcara. Sometimes the angels have other plans; sometimes they simply don't think you are ready or able to make the commitment that is demanded.

If you find that your angel does not want to become an Anamcara, then do not be disappointed or put off. Continue to work with the angels and demonstrate through your own actions that you are worthy of them as an Anamcara.

Remember, in Celtic times the angels only worked with men and women who had dedicated their lives to following a spiritual path. Although we are not living in religious retreats, we need to show something of the same dedication and determination to succeed.

This may seem daunting. And it is. We are souls who have already experienced the cloistered life. Now, in our spiritual progression, we are trying to achieve something more difficult than living the life of a monk or nun: we are seeking to apply the lessons we have learned in past lives to this life—while living in the material world. We are seeking to fulfill our potential of being spirits in the material world.

Sometimes it is difficult to hold on to those spiritual feelings and teachings. Sometimes day-to-day issues threaten to crowd everything else out. But these are the very times when we need the serenity and calm reinvigoration that the spiritual path can bring. And our Celtic Angels and especially our Anamcara can help. They are there for us. Even when we stumble and fall, they will pick us up, dust us down and set us on the track again.

WILL YOU BE MY ANAMCARA?

Sitting at your Angel Altar, light the candles and incense and say your invocation. Sit quietly for a few minutes simply looking at the different elements on your altar. Feel the presence of the Celtic Angels around you. In particular try to sense the personal angel whom you have worked with before. They will probably be standing just behind you and to one side. It is just so easy to imagine you can feel their hand on your shoulder . . .

When you are ready, close your eyes and slowly do the Angel Meditation. When you are floating surrounded by the golden white balls and the Celtic Angels, stop and simply enjoy that sensation.

After a few minutes, when you are ready, feel the landscape changing into a thick wooded forest. You are walking along a narrow path soft with years of dead leaves and pine needles. On both sides of the dark brown path, the undergrowth is thick with ferns and brambles. Bright sunlight speckles the green branches of the trees and bushes all around you. You are content and at peace. As you walk along think of your personal angel and when you are ready call them, using the name you were given.

You should soon feel a presence behind you. Do not turn around, you know it is your personal angel. You reach a clearing. It is small, maybe only thirty feet across. The trees crowd around and as you enter you feel as if you are crossing some kind of threshold. It is warm and sunny here and the tufted grass is pale green and bouncy under your feet. You can see a pair of boulders about two feet high in the middle, ranged like a couple of chairs.

Go and sit on one and then watch as your personal angel sits on the other. You are facing each other. Look at the trees that surround you. There are tall farseeing pine trees, huge lumbering beech trees that hold ancient knowledge, and young bright apple trees that offer choice.

Your future hangs on the decisions you make in this place. But this sacred grove will help you to make the right decisions. This you know. And in this space you can relax.

Greet your personal angel and then, if it feels right, ask them outright if they will be your Anamcara. If you prefer you may wait for them to ask you. But they may not; there is a risk that if you are not sure enough of yourself to ask the question then perhaps they will believe that you are not ready.

Your personal angel may ask you questions about the Anamcara, such as, Do you understand what it means? Are you ready to prove your worth? You must answer these questions honestly. It may well be that you feel nervous about this. But that is only to be expected. If you have serious doubts, this is the time to talk about them. Perhaps you are not ready; there is no shame in that. We all walk different paths through the forest and perhaps you need some more time. To accept that is a powerful lesson in itself.

It is highly likely that your angel will ask you to prove your worth by undertaking some tasks. Usually this will involve committing to daily meditation. I was also asked to give up some of my favorite foods and alcohol. None of the tasks set will be life-threatening, unpleasant or harmful to other living creatures. Nor will they be so hard to do that they are almost impossible. Remember, your Celtic Angels want you to succeed, they are simply looking for some evidence of commitment on your part.

Your personal Celtic Angel should be excited by this and keen to help you. They will suggest a time for a formal ceremony. This will usually be at the time of a Celtic fire festival or the full moon. Though it can be any time, as we have already noted, some days are more powerful than others.

They will take your hand and perhaps for the first time you will feel their touch. As your Anamcara they will always be with you. It will become second nature to you to sense them there beside you. Often at stressful or emotional times you will feel their touch. Remember they are there for you all the time. Always on your side and always wanting the best for you.

When your meeting is over remember to do your closing ceremony. Take a few minutes to think over all that has happened and then write it all down in your Angel Journal.

THE FORMAL CEREMONY

At the time suggested, and perhaps even at an agreed place, do your opening invocation as usual. Then slowly follow the Meeting Your Celtic Angel meditation (see p. 113) until you are sitting facing your Anamcara in the high meadow.

Normally this will be a simple ceremony. They will take your hand and then around you both will gather the white light of love. It will show as a thin circle that flows around you both. Strong positive emotions may well up inside you; do not be alarmed, that is quite natural.

Each ceremony is different but eventually there will come a time that is a natural break and you will feel the draw to return to the material world. Feel yourself drifting back. Say your closing ceremony.

Sit for a few minutes and try to remember that sensation of being joined together. Remember their touch. Cherish the emotions and love that Celtic Angel.

Congratulations! You now have an Anamcara!

Soul Dreaming

Historians and religious commentators make much of the Celtic Church's use of the Anam Cara but I often wonder if they really understand it and give much thought to what the term *soul friend* actually means. The first night after your meeting with your Anamcara, try this exercise. The symbolism is very obvious but it is a beautiful and moving experience.

This is a dream exercise. Do your normal opening ceremony and say your invocation. As you lie in bed, slowly gliding off to sleep, think of your soul flame burning in your heart. Place your hand over your heart and imagine that you can feel its warmth and love as you lie there.

In your dream you are in a vast arid cave; the floor is dry earth and the walls are merely shadows in the distance. There is a gentle golden light, though you can see no source.

You are standing with your hand over your heart. When you take it away a small flame dances there. It is like a butterfly with flames for wings. It is beautiful and you smile and feel happy to see it.

After a moment the butterfly slowly and gently takes off and flies up into the air. As if you are flying with it, you are able to follow it as it gracefully swoops and soars into the cave's highest reaches. You feel the joy and delight it feels as the air supports and nourishes it.

Now you realize that it is dancing. While you can detect no pattern, you just know it is moving to some complicated plan. You smile and laugh as you share its complete enjoyment.

While this is happening you gradually become aware of a sense of presence. When you look around you see another butterfly is flying up to meet you. Or rather your butterfly.

Now the two fly together. Shyly at first, they flow gracefully along, keeping a distance apart. Gradually however, as you watch, the movements become more complex and intricate: they swoop and dive, spiral up and loop back. Also as the movements increase, they spiral around each other in beautiful, languid, intimate patterns of flight. It is as if they leave a trail of sparkling color as they move through the air.

It is such a joy to watch! Now it seems as if the light is intensifying around them, the golden yellow gradually, ever so gradually, increasing. And you feel that light around you as well. Little by little it seems to turn into a fine mist. And all the time the butterflies dance. The lovely golden light now seems to flow over and around you. Like a warm, heavy duvet, you feel it on you. And you are content.

You are now standing on the floor of the cave again, warm and delightfully replete. Your Anamcara is standing beside you. You smile at each other as they take your hand. You feel the coolness and certainty of them as you slowly slip into a deep, refreshing golden slumber.

In the morning remember to do the closing ceremony and then take some time to recall those delightful sensations from the dream. All through the day you should be able to pull those emotions out of your memory and cherish them.

Obviously what is happening here is the meeting of your soul and that of your Anamcara. Don't forget, although they are an angel, just like you they have a soul flame longing to return to the Godhead. With our souls working together, it takes our relationship on to a whole new plane. And while they are helping us to stay on our spiritual path, in some reciprocative way, we, in our stumbling uncertainty, are helping them to succeed too.

Calling on Your Anamcara

Your Anamcara is always with you. You will sense them around you. As you go through your day-to-day life, they are there with you sharing the experiences and emotions that you feel. No relationship is so intimate.

However, you need to have a special time that is just for the two of you. St. Patrick met his angel Anamcara every week and that seems to me to be about right. While it doesn't have to be the same time every week, that is the easiest way to ensure that it happens at all. If you decide to meet your Anamcara every Sunday evening, at least if it doesn't happen one week because you have people visiting, then you can arrange another time. Your Anamcara will understand.

You cannot summon your Anamcara to such a meeting. The two of you need to discuss this in advance and agree that weekly meetings are a good idea. There may even be times when more regular meetings are required.

You can either have this meeting indoors or outdoors. As we have already explained, Celtic Angels prefer as natural an environment as possible. If it feels safe, a perfect option would be to walk along a beach at dusk.

MEETING YOUR ANAMCARA

Do your opening ceremony and say your invocation. Now seek out that inner peace. Let thoughts and impressions flow past until you reach the calm waters of the mountain lake. There you are safe and warm.

Do the Celtic Meditation and when you reach the floating space, pause and enjoy that sensation. Feel the inner calm.

Now become aware, with total certainty, of the presence of someone at your side. And you know it is your Anamcara. You know this for sure. Feel them standing there.

You long to open your eyes, to reach out to them, but restrain yourself. You may feel their hand on your shoulder or around your waist; you may hear their breath as they stand there; you may even smell a sweet scent of lilies. No matter what the sensation is, remain perfectly still and simply welcome them.

Now open your eyes!

It may be that they are standing there. It may be that you see nothing. Either way you will still feel their presence. This is your opportunity to talk about what has happened to you over the past week, ask any questions you have and generally spend time together.

Eventually it will be time to leave your Anamcara and return to your own world. Say your goodbyes, then close your eyes and start your closing ceremonies. When you are ready, open your eyes. Take a few moments to come around and then write down all that happened in your Angel Journal.

Often I do this while I am walking, my Anamcara at my side. You will quickly adapt this meditation to what works best for you. The key point is to create this intimate bond in as vigorous and vibrant a way as possible.

What to Expect from Your Anamcara

The most important thing you should expect from your Anamcara is guidance on how to fulfill your Purpose of Life. This is the lesson you were born to learn. Never forget that your soul chose where to be born because it believed that here was an opportunity, given the way your life was likely to proceed, to experience things it needed to go through in its progression away from the material world and back to the Godhead.

Your Anamcara, because they are more spiritually advanced, is better able to understand the needs of your soul. As your Anamcara's soul dances with yours, it comes to understand and empathize with your own soul and so your Anamcara can help to guide you along your path. Your soul's mission might be, for example, to learn the importance of valuing yourself and trusting yourself to make decisions. If you have low self-worth, then your Anamcara will encourage you to see the positive things about your life and help you to make decisions for yourself instead of always deferring to others.

Because of this, sometimes it may seem as if your Anamcara is not giving you the support that you feel you deserve. This could well be because you need to stand on your own two feet and make the decisions yourself. Remember, if you feel that this is happening to you, your Celtic Angels are always there for you, always there to catch you if you stumble. But you cannot defer all decisions to them; they will not allow that to happen. Ultimately it is your life to lead; all they can do is advise and support.

Your Anamcara relies on you being totally open with them. We have already practiced this but it needs to be stressed. Unless you're totally honest with your Anamcara then any outcome from your discussions will always have an element of doubt. It is easy to imagine a situation where you don't admit to having a phone phobia. You discuss a friend who you feel has been ignoring you and that you're hurt by their behavior. Your Anamcara might suggest that you just pick up the phone and call your friend and ask outright if there is a problem. But because of your phobia, there's no way you're going to do that. You get frustrated at your own inability to do what you've agreed is the right thing, while your Anamcara doesn't understand why you won't act.

Your angels are not completely knowledgeable on all matters. Celtic Angels cannot tell the future. They may understand the big picture better than we do; they are able to see more of any situation than we can and so they perceive the eddies and flows of decisions and their implications better than we can. But they cannot see into the future and tell us what we have to do.

Even in matters spiritual, they do not know all the answers. And if they did they might feel that you would be unable to cope with the answer. I find when questions like that come up, my Anamcara just shrugs or says something noncommittal or even admits he doesn't know.

One such question was over the nature of the Celtic gods. Through meditation and personal experience, I had begun to wonder about the nature of such beings. Were they spirits? Or were they of the earth, perhaps more powerful nature spirits? After one powerful dream, I even began to wonder if they had been created by the Druids themselves to fulfill some role. My Anamcara simply smiled but gave no answer. It took me a while to accept that he simply didn't know.

Working with Your Anamcara on a Day-by-Day Basis

While you will have a weekly meeting with your Anamcara, you will quickly come to recognize their energy at other times as well. You will feel it around you, especially at times of stress or when you are feeling challenged.

Try to acknowledge that presence as much as you can. One way to do this is to carry or wear some memento that reminds you of your Anamcara. When you feel them close by or if you want to call them, finger the memento. As your familiarity grows and the relationship matures, you will find that you need to use meditation less and less to contact them. Often when I am out walking the hills or playing by the ocean, I feel my Anamcara by me. I find now I can talk with him as I would talk with you. And that is very special; you feel honored and somehow worthy of such a delightful experience.

Just recently my partner sent me a text message to say that, for the first time, he had seen my first book, *Walking the Mist*, in a bookstore in Edinburgh. I am not a person driven by ambition. Even when I was at school I always admired people who knew what they wanted to do when they grew up. I've always felt as if I've drifted from one job to another although now, looking back, I can see that I was acquiring all the skills I needed to work as a workshop facilitator and writer.

But the one ambition I always had was to be able to go into a bookstore and buy a copy of my book. Alone, reading my partner's text message, I felt my Anamcara place a hand on my knee and his presence shimmered momentarily at my side. A single tear rolled down my cheek.

To share these special moments is always a joy. To share them with your Anamcara is sublime. You are now much more than simply "you." Your Anamcara means that you are two beings surrounded by Celtic Angels. Together you will learn and grow spiritually. Together you will share and find delight. Together you will succeed!

But there is more! Not only can your personal Celtic Angel act as your Anamcara, but they can help you to access other beings who want to assist you. In the next chapter we go on to examine the importance and potential of working with our ancestors.

TWELVE

Celtic Angels and Your Ancestors

St. Non's is a ruined chapel dedicated to the memory of St. David's mother. It lies just to the west of the city of St. David's, in a sloping field atop a modest cliff on the rugged coastline of Pembrokeshire in southwest Wales. It is a curious site, for the chapel appears to be built north–south instead of the normal east–west; the field itself slopes quite sharply and there is no obvious reason why the ancient monks would have selected this place. As I explored the site I wondered why they would choose such an exposed position when legend states that St. David selected the almost hidden dell for his church precisely because it was invisible from the sea.

It is only when you stand and meditate there that you come to understand more about this place. Surrounding the small ruin there is a ramshackle ring of standing stones. And while it is feeble, there is energy there: a low, even shadow of power. As I stood and connected with the land, the whole area within the circle seemed to lighten up. It was as if the rain had stopped and a golden evening sun was bathing the whole area.

Nearby, at the holy well also dedicated to St. Non, I sat and pondered on all this. Had St. David felt the need to revere his mother? Or was that too literal an interpretation? There are no reliable legends or tales of the two living together and so this site must have been dedicated to her in her absence. It struck me that it showed literally, in stone and mortar, the importance to the Celt of their ancestors. It was all too easy on that rainy night to imagine St. David coming here, retreating from the pressures of his own monastery less than a mile away, and sitting discussing his problems and worries with his deceased mother and perhaps other ancestors as well.

For the Celt, you were what your ancestors made you. You defined yourself as "son of James, son of Michael, son of Nechtan and so on" back nine generations. The standing of your ancestors affected your worth in the community and actions they had undertaken would be remembered in song and narrative down to the present day. It is perhaps not surprising then that the Celts were reluctant to let go of their people once they had died.

Even today, whether we like it or not, we are still very much what our ancestors made us. It amuses me to see how much of my parents is in me, from the way I sit to how I react to situations. They in turn will be very like their parents and so on backwards. So if I was to go back nine generations to each of the 512 people who have contributed something to the person I am today, I would see some similarities to myself. Whether I like it or not! It is a humbling and intriguing thought.

One woman I know discovered that her family was originally from the West Highlands of Scotland. She tells the story of how when she went back to the place she felt immediately at ease, that there was a strange familiarity about the whole area. It was as if she had come home. Many of us experience that sensation without really understanding why.

For the Celt, surrounded by the subtle lives of their ancestors, this impression is not surprising. Indeed there is something instinctive about wanting to return to the place of our birth, or the land of our ancestors. The love of land is so strong and so imbued in us that it flows down the generations, constantly demanding attention until eventually we acknowledge its pull. This doesn't necessarily mean that we pack up and move back. It means that we visit and accept our connections with the land. Perhaps we can get to know some of the locals, help with local charities or simply vacation there every few years. The crucial point is to accept that this piece of land is important to us.

The Celts and Death

In reality we are made up of three parts and when we die the body returns to the earth. The spirit removes itself to the spirit realms and the mind, that part of you that makes you "you," will gradually fade away.

In parts of western Ireland it was believed that on Samhain—Halloween—the dead would leave their graves and return to visit their living relatives. While this might seem like the ultimate horror movie to us, with our ideas of Hollywood zombies and "living dead," to the Irish it was actually something of a celebration. Dead mothers would come to visit their children; husbands to visit their wives; children to comfort their parents. The visitors would sit by the fire and catch up with all the family news, and then, just before dawn, they would return to another year in the cold, damp soil.

This continuity with the past was very important for the Celt. After all, the family was all-important and, as they lived in a world infused with spirits and fairies, it is not surprising that they wanted their dead ancestors to remain part of their world as well.

Death itself was not something that frightened the Celt. In their own day-to-day life they saw how people lived on after their bodies were physically dead. They also believed that the soul, freed from the body, was able to travel forward to the next part of the journey. And of course ultimately to return to the Godhead. Death therefore was something to be celebrated. Today we see this in the dramatic changes at funerals where the emphasis now is often more on a celebration of the person's life than a preparation of their soul for eternity. And perhaps this is how it should be.

In Celtic lands, even today, there is a tradition of having a wake for the dead. This is when everyone gathers and has a party around the coffin of the person who has died. Normally nowadays the coffin will lie in another room and people will take turns sitting with the body while everyone else tells humorous stories about the dead.

Even for the Celt, however, it is hard to accept this joy of death. We have lost that belief, that certainty, in the eternity of the soul, largely because we no longer enjoy that intimacy with the dead that was once so common. To recreate that we must first of all try to find out more about the people who went before us. After that we will look at how we contact these people and then explore how they can help us in our day-to-day lives and our spiritual path.

Finding out about Our Ancestors

Today the family unit has a dramatically diminished role in our lives. It is ironic that at a time when people are living longer and longer we've never known less about our ancestors. While it is not unusual for children to know their great-grandparents, they hear fewer stories about their ancestors. And, in an age of nursing homes and hospices, they have less and less contact with the very old and, indeed, death itself. I myself as a forty-something male have only known two close relatives to die and have never seen a dead body.

There are two obvious ways to try to rediscover our ancestors. The first is to ask people in our family. It might be said that we are all just stories—stories we tell about our own lives and stories others tell about us. These stories will not of course be totally accurate but, nonetheless, even in their exaggerations, they tell us a lot about the people they are describing. Neither do these stories tell us about the day-to-day lives of these persons; rather they tell us about the exceptional events, leaving us to conjure up a picture of the person. I never knew my maternal grandfather, who died before I was born. Yet I have vivid images of him from the tales my mother and her brothers and sisters tell of him. I see him as a real person, a slightly larger-than-life character always with a colorful phrase on his tongue; letting my mother have his dessert, driving a bread van in the days when it was still a horse and cart. Of course there was a lot more to the man. No doubt my grandmother, who died when I was two, could have told of their courting days, of the loving partner and doting father.

The second obvious way is to trace your ancestors through records of birth, marriage and death. Different countries have different ways of recording these momentous events in our lives, but with a little perseverance it is not difficult to go back five or six generations and discover all your ancestors. Or at least discover their names.

In the modern world with the dramatic changes in the way we live our lives and the people we call friends, it is appropriate also to rethink just exactly who we want to call our ancestors. It may be that you have close friends who you know far more about than any members of your family. They may also know more about you. So while there is no blood tie, the emotional tie is much stronger. As a result, after a close friend has died you would want to call on them for counseling and support rather than a family member you know little of and have no feelings about.

MY ANCESTORS

Take a moment to think about your own ancestors. Make a list of people you know from your own family, or close friends, who have died. Like mine, that list may be quite small.

Write down as much of their life story as you can remember. Perhaps there are people still alive who you could ask for more stories. Think in particular of their strengths and weaknesses. Be honest, no one is perfect. If you want to you could create an Ancestors Journal and gather photos or other items that remind you of them.

Try to imagine situations in the recent past when you could have called on this person to help or comfort you. Imagine what you would have said to them and what they would have replied.

The idea behind this exercise is very common, and something you may already have done, albeit not in as intense a manner. Many of us have felt the presence of the recently departed around us for perhaps several days after the event. Talking to them becomes part of the grieving process. My own mother was sitting in church not many weeks after her mother, my maternal grandmother, had died and, as she puts it, she felt someone looking at her. She turned to see who it was and there, sitting at the end of the row, was her own mother. She smiled. My mother was shocked and looked away and then immediately back again but her mother was gone. Nonetheless that visitation gave her comfort and solace and marked for her the end of a period of intense mourning and the beginning of a calmer, more contented acceptance of what had happened. So if we talk to our dead friends and relatives immediately after they die, why not hold on to the memories and talk to them again later?

Many do, of course, and a visit to any graveyard will reveal fresh flowers on numerous old graves. Many visit not just to lay flowers and remember but to talk and discuss with the dead. Sometimes it is just to tell them what has been happening. At other times it might be to ask advice or seek an answer to a question that is troubling the visitor. One old deserted church that I visited in the Lake District hadn't seen a burial in many a year and yet several of the graves were adorned with small bunches of flowers. Straight paths through the overgrown grass told of regular visits. And the overall sense was of the dead at peace and contented. It was strangely reassuring and I felt lighter in step as I left that small refuge.

Celtic Angels and Our Dead Ancestors

It is possible for us to access individual ancestors. Our Anamcara can act as a guide to help us call our ancestors and they will guide and protect us as we work with the memories of our ancestor.

Clairvoyants, mediums and spiritualists all have spirit guides to help them when they communicate with the dead. Our Anamcara and Celtic Angels fulfill a similar role. They are there for us, helping and tending us. And they will prevent us from becoming too emotional or upset by the presence of the dead.

CONVERSATION WITH AN ANCESTOR

To begin with, try to choose an ancestor whom you knew well, someone you got on with and would like to meet again. Discuss this with your Anamcara and make sure you both agree. Sometimes the person you select might not be the most appropriate for your particular stage in your spiritual journey.

When you are ready, select a night and prepare yourself as outlined in Chapter 7. In preparation for this exercise, reread what you wrote about this person in your Ancestors Journal. Try to do as much research as you can. Talk to relatives and friends of the person; find items that were special to them, maybe family heirlooms or just a book or ornament of yours that they liked. Ideally, if they bequeathed anything to you, seek it out. That is very special because not only is it something that they thought enough of to leave to you, it is something that presumably is precious to you because they selected it for you, and that item therefore acts as a bridge between you.

As you are going to sleep try to think about the person and hold their image in your mind. If you find that too difficult, think of the objects you have of theirs or the photos or anything that connects you with them. If you want to ask them a specific question try to keep that in mind as well.

Then, as you sleep, you will meet up with this person. They may have a message for you or take you somewhere. When you wake up, immediately write down everything you can remember.

Once you have done this a few times, you may then start perhaps with older ancestors. It always helps if you have a photograph as this makes it easier for you to visualize them. Little by little you will come to know your ancestors so much better.

My Anamcara warns that the longer a person has been dead, the more difficult it is to make contact with them. Often you end up with just a shell. For eventually our ancestors fade. Whether it is through neglect from us and other people who knew them, or just something that happens, I cannot say. But the memory is not lost entirely, it is just so subtle that only our Celtic Angels can assess it.

The first time I did this I met my step-grandmother who died in 2001. I had never dreamed of her since she had died and now here she was standing at the top of a flight of house stairs. She began to walk down. She was as I remembered her from my youth, not the wizened old woman I had last seen, curled up in her nursing home bed. This was the busy, competent woman I had loved.

We chatted a little and then the dream faded away. I was left with the sense of her contentment, and also her protection and love. It was a lovely sensation. And now we meet regularly and in my dreams I discuss my life and she helps me to find answers to questions that are troubling me.

These are our ancestors, but you need to remember that they are not the people we knew when they were alive. Their body has gone and their spirit has fled. What is left, the mind, is what made them who they were: their outlook on life, their humor, their way of speaking and sometimes an aspect of their emotions as well. Their memory of their own lives may be vague and their awareness of where they are now even vaguer. Nonetheless these memories are very lifelike and helpful to us in our lives.

Working with Our Ancestors

Our ancestors, then, are memories and stories of a person that we can access with the help of our Celtic Angels. As we have already noted, you can talk to a particular ancestor directly, but it is easier to ask the angels to help you. In particular here we are going to learn how to access the ancestors as a collected memory, for we do not necessarily want to access any one person. Rather we want them, all of them, to be there for us. For collectively they are all part of us.

First of all this is something you have to discuss with your Anamcara. You need to think long and hard about whether or not you want to do this exercise. Why do you want to access the ancestors? You also need to define just what you desire. Is it only your ancestors or are there step-parents you would want to involve? Do you have favorite aunts or uncles? What about friends who have died; would you want them to be part of the ancestors as well? It may be that you prefer friends to be separate. Remember, you can access individuals directly.

Once you are ready, there are two times of the year when it is most propitious to hold this ceremony. One is Halloween, obviously; the other is Beltane, the great fire festival on May 1st that welcomes the arrival of summer. This was the fertility festival when people would go out into the countryside a-courting. Nine months later, February 1, is, conveniently, St. Bride's Day, the patron saint of midwives. However, because May 1 was associated with conception, it was believed that the ancestors were present then to supervise the creation of the next generation.

While you can hold this ceremony at any time, those two dates will make it a more powerful experience. Choose dawn on May 1 or dusk on October 31.

Once again you need to collect any family heirlooms you may have, if possible items that were personal to the people involved. Sometimes there are shared family treasures, such as christening gowns or wedding rings. Make a list of your ancestors. Don't worry if it is not complete, but the more names you can add the better.

While it is not essential, it helps the power of the ceremony if you can return to the family homeland and perform this ceremony there. It may be that several pieces of land hold sway with you and your ancestors. In that case ask your Anamcara for their advice. Normally one area of land is much more powerful than any other. If not, you may be advised to visit more than one area.

While you are there take some time, with your Anamcara, to gather some old wood. Oak or chestnut is probably best. Remember, nine generations is about 200 years. Old mature oaks or chestnuts could be 400 to 500 years old, so these are trees that your ancestors could have known as fully grown trees.

Collect some water from a stream or the sea if it is nearby. Your ancestors could well have splashed where you splash; slipped where you slip. Gather some soil or a small rock that seems to call out to you. Find items with strong scents, maybe flowers or pine cones, smells that your ancestors might have enjoyed. Finally, obtain some local plants, perhaps growing wild, that seem appropriate. (Remember to check that these plants are not protected by law before you start digging them up.)

You may well want to take your elements home with you so that you can connect with your ancestors again. That is perfectly fine (keep in mind if you are in another country, however, that customs regulations prohibit bringing back many of these items). All we are doing here is simply gathering material to create a world that the ancestors will feel comfortable in.

YOUR ANAMCARA AND YOUR ANCESTORS

Now you have to give your Anamcara permission to work with your ancestors. Make yourself comfortable and when you are ready, light a candle and say your invocation. Do the full Angel Meditation and then explain to your Anamcara who you want them to find.

This is a conversation that you might want to practice in advance of the ceremony. You also need to think in advance if there are any symbols or items that sum up your family. Generally, landed families have heraldic shields but most of us are not as fortunate, although there are clan totems for most families. Here, however, you just need something to stand as a token for the family.

Assuming that your Anamcara agrees to help you to work with the ancestors, you should present them with your family symbol. This can be a powerful and emotional moment, for there is little more trust we can place in any individual than to open our true family to them.

Your Anamcara will recognize the importance of this gesture as well. As you sit there they may well conjure up a white whirling circle of pure love to surround both of you. Enjoy the preciousness of the moment!

Wait a few minutes. Your Anamcara may want to discuss this in more detail.

Now, together, you will ask your ancestors for help. Be aware of a great silence and of a new presence: a soft, quiet, tired knowledge. This is your ancestors.

Feel the bonds of love that connect you with your ancestors. Feel also their experiences and insights. Without you being aware of it, your Anamcara will be helping you to assimilate the knowledge you need at this point in time. However, for the moment, simply enjoy the connection with the people who made you what you are. You will find at future meetings that you will feel it appropriate to ask particular questions. Again discuss this with your Anamcara first.

When it is appropriate you should begin your closing ceremony. After you open your eyes, wait a few moments and savor that lingering closeness between you and your Anamcara.

You should now place something of your family on your Angel Altar.

Working with Your Ancestors on a Day-by-Day Basis

Sometimes, just occasionally, I will see someone who trails a mist of beings behind them. Like one of those pictures in an exercise book that shows you every step of a yoga or t'ai chi movement, these beings flow after the person as they're walking down the road or serving in a restaurant.

I always thought it was my imagination, but my Anamcara explained that these are ancestors. Either these were people who had always immersed themselves in their family or, like us, they have been working to reacquaint themselves with their dead family members.

Bringing our ancestors into our day-to-day lives is an enriching and ennobling experience. It makes us bigger than we physically are and it also allows us access to a wider set of experiences and emotions.

Tell other people about your ancestors. There are thousands of opportunities every day for us to say to our friends and coworkers, "That reminds me of my grandfather, he used to do that." Or, "My great-aunt was one for the horses, she used to . . ."

What you are doing here is telling tales about the ancestors and as such you are keeping them alive in a way. Think how wonderful it would be for you if, after you are dead, people still remember you fondly and tell tales of your adventures.

Make pilgrimages to where your ancestors used to live. Especially if you have children, this can be exciting and very rewarding as you watch them imagine what life used to be like. And most children have a great curiosity in "Where did I come from?"

Try to remember the individuals on their birthday. When people are alive we usually make a great effort to remember to send them birthday cards. Funny that, once they die, that we forget all about it. Keep their memory. You cannot send them a card but you could visit their grave or even just put their photo on your Angel Altar. That way you can involve your Celtic Angels in your remembering of them.

You can walk with the person. To do this you need to imagine that they are there beside you. I find the easiest way to do this is to mark out a clear start and finish. You might start by sitting in a park bench. Do the Angel Meditation and then, with your Anamcara there, and with your eyes still shut, invite your ancestor to sit beside you. Try to sense them there. Imagine how they would appear and how they would feel to you.

Open your eyes and get up without looking and start walking. Imagine that they are there at your left shoulder. Maybe they are walking a step behind. Talk to them as you would to any other person.

To begin with you may feel a little daft. I certainly did. But if you do this several times, trying to replicate exactly what you did before, the sense of someone being there grows each time. Of course, with the possible exception of the most recently deceased, your ancestors have lost their awareness of corporeal presence and so this is your imagination creating this entity. However, you are opening up an avenue for the ancestor to communicate directly with you. And you will quickly realize that the replies you are hearing, the ideas and opinions being expressed are not ones you would normally experience. That is when the whispers are being heard by your subconscious and translated into your head. That is when you have made contact with your ancestor.

Mostly, however, you merely want to create a sense of the ancestors being around. They are a resource that your Celtic Angels can draw on to help you succeed. This is a bank of knowledge and experience that we can tap into and to see how others coped with the problems and dilemmas we now face.

Perhaps you have been offered a job in another part of the country. Should you accept it? Should you uproot your family or leave them here and only see them on weekends? Perhaps your partner doesn't want to go; should you put career ahead of love and family? These are all perfectly reasonable questions and ones that many of your ancestors must also have faced. How did they choose? Did they regret their choice or was it completely vindicated by what came next? And because part of them is in you, it makes their experience even more valuable to you.

So working with the ancestors can be highly rewarding and informative. It can help you to make the decisions that need to be made and to appreciate what you really feel about any situation. Tended by your Celtic Angels, the ancestors make you more than you are. They give you a perspective and understanding that others don't have. They enrich your life, root you in the past and give you the insight you need for the future. But they are not the only help we have in the spirit world. Our soul family are also there for us. And in the next chapter we explore how they too can enrich and expand our lives.

THIRTEEN

Celtic Angels and Your Soul Family

The golden sands of Belhaven Bay near Dunbar sweep off to my left as I stand looking north out over the icy cold blue water of the Firth of Forth. The kingdom of Fife is just a dark blur on the winter horizon and I shiver despite my many layers of clothing. It is a cold January morning in southeast Scotland.

I am standing at the very edge of the sea and it is as if my awareness changes. No longer am I confined to my body. No longer am I merely a mortal man marveling at the natural world. Now, I realize, I am part of it. As I feel myself flow out over the water, it seems as if the wind abates, and even the chill retreats. Now I am a primitive force, an energy, courted by the elements.

Then, just for a second, I felt the connection. So slight, so fleeting that it might never have happened, yet so profound that I know it did. I felt the connection to my other soul brothers and sisters.

It is the only time I have been so aware of them. These soul brothers and sisters are kindred souls who, like me, are part of a greater soul being. For although a flame burns within my heart, it is only one of many who make up my family. Together we share experiences and knowledge, learn our lessons and feel the draw of the Godhead.

This family is one of the most amazing aspects of life today, for it is a voluntary arrangement among spirits able to trust and love each other. None of us can escape to the Godhead until all of us are ready.

You may think that your own Anamcara could be part of your soul family. After all, it would be in their own interest to help us. But that is not the case. Even in today's highly mobile technological world it is hardly likely you would meet any of your soul family as it is not in any of the souls' interest to share experiences.

Some people have postulated that when you establish a rapport with a complete stranger it is because they are of your soul family. Again, that is possible but unlikely. To start with, if each family is made up of some twenty-five souls, maybe twelve of them would be in the world at any one time. What are the chances of meeting one out of twelve out of 5 billion?

Secondly, there is a far more convincing argument which is that these people are actually souls with whom you have had some form of relationship in a past life. And it is that connection that you are recognizing now. To me that is more probable. One thing I have noticed talking to lots of people about their past lives is that we seem to return to the same culture again and again. It is not totally exclusive and we do seem to move on but, for example, you meet lots of people who have had past life experience in Egypt and then maybe Rome and then Celtic lands. There seems to be a sort of Western European/Eastern Mediterranean grouping.

So it is possible that each member of a soul family specializes in one area, one people. As they live life after life in, say, a Celtic environment, not only will they learn their lessons, they will experience and possibly even cause the ebb and flow of the culture and collective awareness of the people themselves. They will appreciate the most subtle aspects of a way of life that may take many lives to comprehend.

This might seem quite difficult for us to accept today. We are used to thinking of ourselves as individuals. In the modern Western world we think very much of me, me, me. Even parents, while they may put their children first, are nowadays aware that they too should have their own lives and have desires and ambitions that do not necessarily focus around their family.

For the Celts all this would be fantastic. They were raised within the family and their every action was considered in terms of whether or not it benefitted the family. Marriages were arranged, trades were selected, lives were organized around the needs of the family. From our perspective today, it would seem a very oppressive environment where any individual desires or longings would have had to have been suppressed.

Such communal living for the Celts was the norm and they rejoiced in the continuity, support and shared knowledge that such a system brings. There is indeed great comfort and solace in being part of a greater group where all major decisions are taken for you and where ritual and ceremony cover your every action.

Celts would therefore not have found it so difficult to consider themselves part of a greater soul family as well. Unlike the biological family, the soul family makes no demands whatsoever. Rather it is a resource, a library of experience and knowledge that, if we know how, we can draw on to help us through our own lives and to fulfill the spiritual tasks we set ourselves before we were born.

Celtic Angels can help us to achieve this. Our Anamcara is only too aware of the soul family and can help us to access it and understand the results of our contact. Again this is a very personal issue and one we have to treat with great care. Our

Anamcara cannot approach the collective awareness of the soul family on our behalf, only we can do that. All our Anamcara can do is to empower and guide us.

Becoming Aware of the Soul Family

Often events occur that only our subconscious picks up on. Our Western materialistic, organizing brain is busy worrying about problems, running our calendars and keeping everything going. It doesn't have time to explore emotions and feelings. So our subconscious has to alert us to these subtle influences that flow around us. It cannot do so by talking to us directly as those functions are controlled by the rational brain. It therefore has to use other means: images, emotions, notions, even dreams.

An example of this was one day when I was at the Port of Whithorn on the Galloway coast in southwest Scotland. There, an ancient ruined chapel stands on the point overlooking the entrance to the harbor and while the stone building is thought to date from the Middle Ages, the site itself is much more ancient. It may even be the original site of the Candida Casa, the original monastery in Scotland built by St. Ninian probably in the early fifth century. I entered the site and immediately sensed the great power of the place. As I meditated, however, the ground began to sway and I started to feel sick. As I fell to my knees a great voice boomed out, "Get out of here! Get out of here!" The anger and hatred in it was so profound that I felt real terror as I crawled free of the building.

But this was not some evil demon. My Anamcara explained later that the energy there was either too strong or too incompatible with me in some way so that my subconscious, realizing this, reached around in a panic to find a way to warn me. This was how it succeeded in getting me out of that place. It projected emotions, perhaps remembered from an old film or subconscious fears, which my materialistic brain picked up on and transferred into what seemed the most appropriate form. Perhaps now, years later, if I went back I would be okay.

So it is with our soul families. The connection between us, while we are alive, is faint and is not intended to be used at all. As we have already said, shared experiences are a waste of resources as far as our soul families are concerned. However, becoming aware of those connections can give us great comfort and also help us to appreciate our own role more and how we connect with everyone else; how our material and spiritual beings are linked. Putting it bluntly, if we hurt or behave badly towards another, how can we be sure they are not part of our soul family?

THINKING OF OUR SOUL FAMILY: A VISUALIZATION

Visualization exercises can sometimes be good ways of appreciating a teaching, especially when we want our subconscious to be alert to the subtle flows that exist around us.

Find a quiet, peaceful place and take a few minutes simply to sit and become calm. Light a candle and do your invocation. When you are ready, do the Celtic Meditation and then float gently, letting the thoughts flow past you.

Sense your Anamcara standing beside you.

Feel the whirl of the Celtic Angels as they dance around you.

Now look inward and seek inner calm. Feel the tranquillity flow over you and enwrap you in a warm blanket of love. Feel a soft, sleepy darkness descend on you and now, when you are ready, feel yourself drifting off.

You are walking across a great grassy plain. The sky is a warm pale blue and the grass is a gentle green color. It is thick and soft underfoot. It is flat as far as you can see in any direction and you feel a lightness of spirit that only comes in such places.

Ahead of you, you can see a globe about the size of a soccerball floating in the air about three feet off the ground. As you approach you realize that it is an image of the earth. As you see this, all around you grows dark and now you are floating above the earth.

Find where you are on the planet. Look for the small flame of your spirit. As you fall towards the earth you will see its faint flickering beauty. Feel a deep sense of love as you look at it.

Floating there connecting with your own soul flame, slowly you will become aware of other pulls. As you float up again to see the whole earth, notice here and there other small pulses of light. Feel the gentle contented love of the souls. Close your eyes in your visualization and sense the earth there below and these beacons of love from your soul brothers and sisters.

You are loved. And you love. What could be greater?

When you are ready, prepare to close down. In your visualization slowly feel yourself drifting away from the globe until you are back on the vast plain. Begin to remember where you are meditating, feel your body around you. When you are ready, open your eyes and do your closing-down ceremony.

This is a fabulous visualization but it can be very powerful. Take a few minutes to readjust to your world. In your Angel Journal remember to record the emotions you felt as you realized the implications of linking with other beings all over the planet.

Feeling the Touch of Our Soul Family

Our Celtic Angels are our inspiration and also our teachers. As they whirl around us they remind us that we need to relate more to the spiritual side of our existence than most of us do today in our plastic neon world. The Celtic Angels are also the key to appreciating our soul family.

The last visualization helped us to understand the nature and implications of being part of a soul family. This I find exciting and also a little humbling. Now we are going to reach out to the accumulated knowledge and experience that our soul families have. In preparation for this meditation you need to pick a date and time. Discuss it with your Anamcara and listen to what they have to say to you. You will find that a time will come to you that you know is the correct time to do this exercise.

In the week before, each day at the agreed time, light a candle and sit quietly trying to imagine what it will be like to become aware of your soul family. Remember the visualization and the emotions it engendered in you. Revel in them again. Try to imagine the different experiences and ways of looking at life that each member of your soul family will hold. Contemplate how becoming aware of such knowledge will change your life. For it will.

This meditation works best either on a hill or a mountain top. Failing that, you need somewhere with wide open space and a real sense of being able to stretch to the very horizons of the land. For it is that sense of being able to reach out beyond our physical body and flow to the far distance, just as I experienced at Belhaven Bay, that we now want to cultivate.

CONTACTING OUR SOUL FAMILY

On the day you have chosen, find a spot where you feel comfortable. Now stand facing east. Make your invocation and when you are ready close your eyes. Do the Angel Meditation and then, when you are surrounded by golden balls of energy and Celtic Angels, pause.

Call your Anamcara to you. Feel them standing behind you. Perhaps you will feel their touch. Enjoy that wonderful moment for what it is.

When you feel ready tell your Anamcara that you want to reach out to other members of your soul family. And ask for their help.

Feel the golden energy inside you and feel it change into a misty white. Sense it lightening and thinning as it does. You feel lighter and lighter until you are rocking on the balls of your feet and you feel as if you could simply rise up like an angel's feather and drift off on the wind. Just at that very last moment as your feet seem certain to leave the ground, feel the energy seep out through the crown of your head and flow slowly up into the sky.

As it does feel your awareness rise with it. Be aware of the ground falling away from under you and look down at the distant lands. Now you are standing on the hilltop and rising far above it. On the hilltop feel the presence of your Anamcara. They may well speak to you at this point, whispering in your ear. Listen to what they are saying. As they do this, you will become aware of other beings far distant.

Through all your preparations and through your work with your Anamcara they will have become aware of your calling. Even if they do not understand what is happening they will have grasped, perhaps at an instinctive, deep subconscious level, that you are seeking them out. They will make time for you.

High above the ground as you float surrounded by Celtic Angels languidly circling you, try to free your mind of all thoughts. Simply be. Sense the cool air around you, the sun on your face, the faint dampness that the high clouds bring. Feel the earth far below and the deep calming knowledge of the trees from near and far. Bathe in this world of peace and love and simply let your consciousness drift as it will.

Eventually you will once again become aware of standing on the hilltop. Faint memories and impressions of your meditation will remain and once you have completed your closure, try to remember as much as you can and write it down. Most likely it will be scraps of images: vaguely remembered places, panoramas, rooms, streets, rolling countryside. These are impressions gathered from other members of your soul family. For days afterward you might keep remembering snippets.

Having opened up to the influence of your soul family, you will find changes in your own perspective. You might discover that you are drawn to news items about various countries or regions. You might feel a strange draw to visit a place you had never thought of traveling to before. Even the plight of people

or animals that previously you might have felt pity for, will motivate you more and you may well find yourself drawn to working with specific charities.

These changes are to be welcomed. They are all part of the changing, more aware, more compassionate you. Celebrate! You are working well with your Celtic Angels and becoming more aware of your spiritual identity and its needs and desires.

Working with Your Soul Family Day by Day

Once you have opened up to the subtle energies of your soul family, it becomes much easier to appreciate them day by day. You may have soul family anywhere and at any level of development. They may not all be human, some may be animals or even plants. So as you open up to your soul family, you are in a small way opening up to the universe. This can be a daunting thought. The worlds that surround us are so vast and so complex we cannot possibly comprehend them all. Don't even try to. Simply attempt to be more compassionate to everyone and everything. Try to be aware of everyone else's life, desires and fears, and help them as best you can.

It is highly unlikely that you will be able to make contact with any individual soul family member currently alive. Our partners and lovers are almost certainly not part of our soul families. As has already been noted, it is actually not desirable for kindred souls to meet.

Plato talked about love being two sides of a being coming together to create one. He argued that when this occurred it was possible to rise above base material desires and to appreciate a greater, more creative, more spiritual form of relationship. From this we get the idea of soul mates and platonic love. Remember, however, the soul family is an agreement made purely between souls where material matters, such as love or desire, or even personality, are of no interest.

In all this you need to remember that you are an individual with needs and desires as well. It is too easy to turn all your focus outside yourself and dedicate your whole existence to working with others.

One way to contain this is to set aside specific time to work with your soul families, maybe one day a month, or even just one day a year. On that day, you would seek contact once again with your soul family and, working with your Anamcara, work out plans for the following period. You are an advanced spiritual being and you have spiritual work you need to achieve in this lifetime too. It could even be that *this* is the lesson you need to learn!

Learning to Use the Wisdom of Your Soul Family

Your Celtic Angels, and in particular your Anamcara, are the spirits you should always work most closely with. They are there to help you and to see that you achieve your Purpose of Life. Their main concern, however, is your spiritual well-being. Sometimes your ancestors can be helpful because their experience and knowledge can help you to cope with much more materially based problems and even just their presence can be a comfort as you go through the daily routines of life.

When you choose to work with your soul family, however, it is different. The awareness you gain is very subtle. Often you will not even be aware of having received any knowledge at all; it is a subtle emotion or an idea that suddenly appears. This is why it is best to work with your Anamcara on this, as they can point out the teaching you have experienced.

Generally it will either be a general point or it might show you how to find a solution to problems that perhaps have never occurred before in your family. Your ancestors would not be able to help you with this particular difficulty.

In Scotland in the early nineteenth century we saw a period of rapid agricultural change that has become known as the Clearances. In this time vast tracts of land were turned over by the lairds to sheep grazing. The traditional crofting villages were wiped out and families removed from their ancestral lands, their houses burned to the ground. In the parish church of Croick, north of Inverness, scared and half-starved Highlanders cowered, seeking shelter. In a grotesque parody one of them scratched into the church window: "Glencalvie People the wicked generation Glencalvie." Even today people come to this desolate monument to the greed of humans and weep.

Nothing like this had ever happened to these people before. The laird, the clan chief, was supposed to look after and protect them. The people had no one to turn to for advice and so when they were offered passage to America or Australia, what choice did they have?

Standing there in that forsaken place, it is difficult not to feel anger and fury. Yet as I reach back through my ancestors I sense nothing but acceptance. Though this was not my land, we were all Celts together. My Anamcara reminds me that anger is a futile emotion, which destroys and does not create. Then he reveals a sense from my soul family. A complex emotion flows over me. It is calming, but more than that it makes me feel as they did and how even in that darkest of moments there was still hope. Strange half-formed echoes surround me and ideas I can't quite grasp nonetheless tug at my emotions and I feel the anger slip away. It is replaced with an awareness that such things happen and that many of the people, though desolate, would recover and go on to achieve great things in America, Canada, Australia and New Zealand.

With your Anamcara you can turn your awareness outward and become alert to the plight of the worlds around you. You should try, whenever you can, to pause for a moment and let your awareness seep out across the land.

Now you have met your Celtic Angels. You have welcomed and worked with your Anamcara. Through the angels you are able to access the knowledge of the ancestors and your soul family. These are great achievements. From now on you will never be alone and your spiritual awareness will always be heightened.

There are many ways in which your Celtic Angels can help you to enrich and broaden your life experiences. In the next part we move on to examine some of the gifts they can offer you and how, ultimately, they can help you to find the reasons why you were born.

PART THREE

Bringing Angelic Attributes into Your Life

FOURTEEN

Celtic Angels
and the Land

Until now we have concentrated on those Celtic Angels who have been drawn to work with humans. These beings are drawn to people like ourselves who are opening up to the spiritual aspects of our life and seeking to understand more about our role here on earth and how best we can seek to fulfill our destiny.

There is another group of Celtic Angels too. These are spirits who have not eschewed the world of humans but rather are drawn to work with particular sacred sites. Unlike most of the spirits who flock to these sites, these Celtic Angels are happy to work with humans who are attracted to the same place. Often the Celtic Angels are there for similar reasons to us and so by helping us work through the issues we need to address they presumably help themselves as well. Alternatively, it may be that they had real problems when they were human and so are keen to help others to avoid all the mistakes they made. It is also my experience that these angels tend to be more advanced spiritually than even my Anamcara. He was as in awe of them as I was.

Whatever the reason, these angels are there and by approaching them correctly and respecting their own needs, we can work with them and help our spiritual journey. Indeed the first Celtic Angel I came across was at a site near where I live. As I have already mentioned there is a spot by the river where it bends very slightly. I have always felt that the spot never looked quite right. And for that reason I was drawn to it again and again. Eventually I realized what was happening and started to meditate there. Almost immediately I saw with my mind's eye that the site used to be different. There used to be a large boulder and the river flowed around it, creating a small bubble of land. Presumably at some time the boulder had been removed and now the river has no reason to bevel.

Quickly thereafter I encountered the Celtic Angel of this site. He appeared at first in my mind's eye and then later in front of me, but laughed when I called him an angel.

"I am no angel!" he said.

"What are you then?" I asked. "What should I call you?"

After a long silence, he smiled. "To you I suppose I am an angel. But to me, I am simply me, with no need to name what I am."

Somehow it never seems appropriate to ask a Celtic Angel why they are at a particular site. Often I would plan to ask this reluctant angel, but once there the idea would simply go out of my head. Then afterward I would kick myself and pledge that I would ask him the next time. But I never have.

In this chapter, then, we are going to look at how to work with Celtic Angels who are visiting sacred sites.

How Do You Find a Site?

Sacred sites are special places where there is an energy that helps us to meditate and access the spiritual realms. It could well be that the energy is something measurable, such as radioactivity given off by granite or radon gas or some other kind of physical emissions. It may be something that can be seen, like colors or shape of the land; or it may be something psychic, some kind of power that is generated at a level that we cannot yet truly understand.

Its importance is that it works. Ancient humans understood it when they built their stone circles and tombs; Druids understood it when they advised on the building of castles and even villages; and Celtic saints understood it when they chose sites for their monasteries and hermitages. There is magic in the land.

Like the ancient Celts, when we start to meditate and appreciate the spiritual aspects of the natural world we quickly become aware of the existence of these sites. Without understanding why, we get drawn to some places rather than others. Even in your own home you will have found that, somehow, it just seems right to do your angel work in particular rooms. We simply need to accept this and not worry too much about why it happens.

FINDING SACRED SITES

You may not realize it but you are surrounded by sacred sites. Even in towns and cities there are places that retain something of their magic. Some sites will be more powerful than others. Some will draw you while others will not, and some may even repel you. In this exercise you are simply going to understand what in fact you already know: that you live in a special place.

Sit in a space where you feel comfortable and take a few moments to settle and calm your breathing. When you are ready, light your candle and say your invocation. Just watch the candle flame for a few minutes and as you do so think of your own sacred flame flickering deep inside your heart.

Now close your eyes and concentrate on your breathing. Feel it slowing down and deepening as you gradually relax.

When you are totally calm and facing inward, do the Celtic Meditation. When you are a being of light floating in a gentle cloud of peace, pause and enjoy that moment.

Now be aware that with your mind's eye you can see in the brown and red colors the outline of clouds. As you concentrate feel the clouds slowly become more real until you can see them quite clearly.

You are floating above a bank of fluffy white clouds. You know that if they parted, you would be able to look down on the land around your own house. The land you know so well. The land that called you home.

Slowly sink down until you are surrounded by the gray-white mist of these clouds. Feel the cool dampness on your skin. Sense the land so far below. Gradually the gray-white mist is clearing. To begin with you can only see glimpses of the land, then longer snatches and then eventually it clears altogether. It feels as if you are in an airplane looking down. Traveling fast yet not traveling at all.

Now it seems as if a darkness comes over the land. Only it is not clouds or changes in the weather, it is as if you have slipped on dark sunglasses. The land is now in black and white, the edges clear but muted somehow. And then you see some spots are marked in red. Small red circles. These are the sacred sites. You feel a rising excitement inside. These are spots that are being pointed out to you. Try to remember as many of them as you can.

All too soon the clouds begin to gather again and soon you are floating in a dark cloudy mist. It is time to return.

Refocus your mind and feel your body around you. Take a few moments and when you feel ready open your eyes. Make your closing ceremony and then sit for a few moments recapturing what you have just seen.

Quickly write down all that you can remember in your Angel Journal. You may be surprised that despite the preciseness of the map when you were looking at it, now you may only remember impressions rather than precise directions. Don't worry, that happens.

You may want to visit these sites. At a workshop in Glasgow a woman told me that she had visited many stone circles and other such sites and while she had sensed the beauty and holiness of them, nothing special had resonated with her. Sacred sites need to be seen like tools: they are there to help you in your spiritual work, but like all tools you need to know how to use them.

Once you have appreciated that there are lots of sites around where you live, the next stage is to select one to visit. Not all sites have Celtic Angels associated with them, at least in my experience. Some sites might be good for you to visit and work with anyway and your Anamcara should help you to decide where to go. Some sites, however, are clearly associated with Celtic Angels and it may be that you are drawn to visit them.

St. David's in southwest Wales is an ancient site. Although there is some debate about whether the cathedral is indeed built on the original site of the monastery, it is a special place. There, walking around the small cathedral with its sloping floor, there was a real sense of this being a holy place, of this being something exceptional.

As I sat and meditated I became aware of two Celtic Angels who appeared with an old chest. They opened it and produced a large white sheet which they pulled out until it covered a fair space in the small chapel where I was sitting. I have no idea what that meant but I hope that one day it will become clear. Perhaps it stands for purity, or an adventure not yet written?

Many of the sites that angels visit are not generally known. I have found as I travel around the Celtic lands that many stories exist of angels but they are only known locally. The first step is to ask your Anamcara. They are more open to the subtle energies than we are and so may be able to recommend sites angels are more likely to frequent. Equally, when you are at a site they might alert you to the presence of a Celtic Angel.

There are other more practical steps you can take. You can seek out sites where Celtic saints communed with angels.

It is often a moot point whether the saint or the angel came first. Sites such as Croagh Patrick and Carningli are ones where the angels almost certainly attracted the saints and not the other way around.

In other cases sites are mentioned in the hagiographies of the saints, such as the Fairy Hill of Iona or the small island of Farne. Third, there are sites specifically mentioned in the old legends and sagas of the Irish, sites such as Tara and possibly Armagh. There is sometimes a debate as to their precise location.

Finally, you can use your own intuition. If you are open to the flow around you and if you are meant to meet another Celtic Angel then, by following your intuition, you will.

When You Are at a Site

When you approach a site that you know is associated with Celtic Angels there is obviously a great sense of anticipation. You hope the angels will appear to you and that you will be inspired and also receive some profound message. That, however, is not always the case. Even if nothing happens you should not be downhearted but enjoy the beauty and energy of the site.

The first time I visited Carningli in Pembrokeshire, I had no idea what to expect. I had read about the hill in several different places but had never seen a clear photo. Even the detailed map I had ended slightly to the west of the summit.

The first lesson I have long learned is that you should never just arrive at a site. You need to approach it on foot and with intent in your heart. I therefore chose to walk from a parking lot about two miles from the hill. Given the intermittent torrential downpours, I confess to regretting this decision. But I had been guided to park there by my Anamcara and so accepted that.

It was a gentle walk across raised moorland. And almost immediately there was a sense of presence. There were piles of stones that might have been cairns or simply abandoned scree from the retreating ice sheets. Large boulders could have been standing stones. All around there was a sense of mystery.

By the time I arrived at the piles of scree and ragged crags that make up the summit of Carningli, I was soaked to the skin but also totally inspired. The sense of wilderness and unspoiled beauty that greets you there is quite breathtaking.

Legends say that the local saint, St. Brynach, came here to commune with his angels and so I set off to try to find where he might have sat. Of course it was 1,500 years ago and the site had been much visited; who knows what changes might have been made? However he would have been attracted by some kind of energy. I did find a semi-cave formed by a large flat boulder jutting out from a steep pile of scree but there was no real feeling about that spot. Some legends say that he went to a ruin of a fortress but I saw no such there. At least, now that I think about it, nothing that was so obvious.

In sites where there is a regular design, for example a stone circle or in the bend of a river, then it is fairly clear where the powerful center is. In hill sites it is less so. You cannot assume that it is necessarily on the crown of the hill. Elva Hill in the Lake District has a stone circle on its southern flank and Doon Hill in East Lothian similarly has an ancient temple site on its southeastern side.

One simple exercise to find the special spot is to stand as close as possible to where you think the source of power is. Make sure you are facing east. Say your invocation and focus in on yourself. Clear your mind and concentrate on your breathing. Take several minutes until you feel totally calm and at peace.

Slowly imagine roots, like plants roots, coming out from the soles of your feet and growing down into the ground.

Unlike the Celtic Meditation, do this very slowly, inch by inch. Once they are about nine inches into the ground, stop. Try to sense the land around you. Then simply let your roots expand as they will. Let them flow long and smoothly. Your roots will be drawn to the source of the spiritual energy in any place, however diffused it is. In a perfect location they will fan out around you, indicating that you are standing right on top of the source. In other cases they will flow in different directions.

At Carningli I was led to a particular boulder that formed a comfortable seat. In front another stone rose up and in my mind I immediately called it the pulpit. And it was there that the Celtic Angels came to me.

Celtic Angels who belong to sites inspire simply by their presence. For them the world of humans is distant and of little consequence; nonetheless they can intervene when they choose to.

Communicating with the Celtic Angels

You need to be aware that the Celtic Angels may not always simply talk to you. In some cases these beings are too ethereal and divine to do so. Instead they may communicate with you by actions or by using nature or even emotions.

My own experience at Carningli illustrates this. I was sitting at the "pulpit," with my eyes closed, deep in meditation. I had done the Angel Meditation and was just floating surrounded by golden balls of energy. My Celtic Angels were swirling around, when I had an urge or command to open my eyes. When I did, five huge opaque figures were progressing across the sky. Indeed at first I thought they were sunbeams.

Somehow my mind knew they were more than that and as I followed their serene procession, I could see the shapes of their bodies very lightly defined. These beings must have been fifty feet or more in height. I watched them for at least five minutes until they slowly faded away. I even had the notion that they were carrying something but I don't know what.

Strange unnamed emotions swept through me and I knew I had been privileged to see something so incredible, even if I didn't understand what it was exactly.

Within minutes, however, I was beginning to doubt what I had experienced. My logical Western brain was kicking in and explaining it all away. It was my imagination: I had dearly wanted to see something special at Carningli and so I had taken what were sunbeams, a perfectly natural phenomenon, and imbued them with hints of shapes to suit my needs. By the time I had started to climb around the hilltop to return the way I had come, I had more or less convinced myself.

And then there, clustered around another outcrop of jagged boulders, were the same five sunbeams. I couldn't believe it. Somehow I knew they were saying to me that they could prove they were real. And the proof lay where they were gathered.

This outcrop, Carn Edward, had called out to me on the walk to Carningli but it had been raining hard and I had just wanted to get to the summit. More than that, it had seemed to me at first that it was an old ruin and it was only when I had got closer that I had realized that it was totally natural.

Once I reached the boulders I could see there were two quite distinct piles. In the eastern one there was a large flat stone such as Celtic saints favored for meditating on. I wondered if this was what I had been shown by the Celtic Angels. Somehow I sensed it was not. I stood on that stone and tried to open up to the energies of the site, seeking something, I knew not what.

I was shown a spot around the back of the other pile. As I scrambled around, the rain came again and I started arguing with myself once more, saying I was on a fool's errand. Clearly I wasn't going to find graffiti saying, "Brynach was here," nor was I going to find a secret chest or whatever. Thousands, if not hundreds of thousands of people have passed this way since his time. Anything less, I argued, would not be conclusive proof.

In the event, I stood looking at a large upright stone with a ledge along the top. Half-heartedly I checked the crevices at the side but saw nothing. Then suddenly an owl peeked over the top of the boulder, its round, bold white face making it seem even more startled than it must have felt. It looked down at me and then launched into silent flight. This is exactly the unexpected thing that Celtic Angels would use to let you know you had been led there. Not only is it highly unusual to see an owl during daylight hours, or perched on stones, but, perhaps even more importantly, for the Celt the owl was seen as a messenger between the spirit and human worlds. Clearly the angels were sending me a message. All my earlier doubts left me and it was as if I lived the sighting of the Celtic Angels again. Standing there in the pouring rain, I thanked the angels for this wonderful day and walked back to the car with a spring in my step.

When you leave any sacred site, but especially one that is associated with Celtic Angels, you should always take time to write up your journal. Try to think of everything that happened, thoughts you had, sights you saw, anything unusual or unexpected. You might have been drawn to particular spots, or felt emotions rare for you.

Sometimes we are not open enough for the Celtic Angels, or we are too preoccupied or we are concentrating on experiencing something to the exclusion of the real sensations, which pass us by. Take time to replay it all and see what you remember.

Working with the Celtic Angels at Sacred Sites

There is a question that you need to answer. Why do you want to communicate with these Celtic Angels? What is it they can do that will help you in your spiritual journey? For me at Carningli, I needed a dramatic experience with the Celtic Angels to reassure me that the work I was doing was valuable and that this book, being written while I was there, was the right thing for me to undertake.

Sometimes your Anamcara and your own Celtic Angels simply aren't enough. Perhaps they don't have the necessary insights or are too close to you.

Whatever the reason, you need to understand your motivation before you visit any site. Always consult your Anamcara too. They can help you to make the correct decisions.

As different sites have different energies, so they attracted people with quite different needs. St. David's in Wales, for example, was the site chosen by an ascetic monk for his monastery. What was there in that site that appealed to him? And would any Celtic Angels drawn to that site feel similarly?

The church site at Kilmore lies about four miles southeast of Oban on the Scottish west coast. The original church was built there by St. Beone because an angel appeared and told him this was the site for his church. In fact it was almost certainly an ancient pagan site before. The energy in that space is very old and reverent. The whole countryside there is riddled with ancient monuments, standing stones and other neolithic sites. To meditate there is to feel the gentle pull of a lazy river on a summer's day. It is cool and sleepy, calming and almost dreamlike in its inspiration.

So if you are drawn to one of these sites you need to wonder why. Remember these Celtic Angels are probably from the second level and so their insights will be highly spiritual. There is no point going to one of them for help in paying your gas bill. As in all pilgrimages it is useful to formulate a question in advance and to keep it constantly at the front of your mind, chanting it to yourself like a mantra.

Visiting a sacred site with your Celtic Angels is a very special experience. It is probably the nearest we can come to experiencing the spiritual realms. While these sites are not necessarily gateways to the other realms, they may well be windows and the knowledge we gain there can help us in our resolution to take control and direct our own lives for our greater spiritual good.

You can visit sites as often as you want. However in the busy modern world that is not always possible. Certainly to begin with each visit should be special, anticipated and planned. You may find that one site calls out to you and you find yourself making the time to go back again and again. You might feel the need to start tending the site, or planting some flowers, or renovating an old well. Rejoice if that happens: there are few greater honors than becoming a guardian of a sacred site.

Of course you may just want to go to the site and enjoy the serenity and holiness of the place. That is fine. That is great. Go there, meditate and enjoy! Take a picnic, but remember always to spill a little liquid on the land and leave a share for the Celtic Angels.

FIFTEEN

Celtic Angels Can Inspire

At my workshops, we rely a lot on Celtic music, both traditional and modern. I am constantly fascinated by how the images and the emotions conjured by the music can vary so much from person to person. Why is it that when we view a painting or admire a work of art, some people will adore it while others, although they appreciate the workmanship, remain untouched by it? Collect any group of people together and ask them to chose their favorite poem or traditional tale and it is rare that people will agree on which is the best.

I feel we all appreciate creative works in different ways because both the created works of art and the very art of creation are sacred. More than that, it is as if the Celtic Angels who inspired the artist have included a message that speaks not only to our conscious selves but to the divine spark that resides within.

Taliesin, the great sixth-century Welsh poet, when he wanted to compose a special poem, would retreat to a cave high in the hills. There, in the darkness, he would commune with the world of spirits to seek inspiration and ideas for his composition. Adomnán, St. Columba's seventh-century biographer, tells us that in the last days of the Saint's life, the angels taught him many new spiritual songs, which he sang and had never been heard before. Taliesin and St. Columba, in doing this, were following a long tradition of druidic and Christian thought that saw the great works as being, at least in part, messages from the Celtic Angels.

This combination of human experience and spiritual insight was thought to be crucial in the creation of a work of art that would entertain, educate and inspire the Celts. Remember that humans may well be unique in their ability to perceive the divine. Yet we remain trapped within the material world. How beautiful then to be able to bring some of that divine into our lives, for not only do we revel in it, it reminds us of our ultimate spiritual goal.

So we can say that for anyone who is seeking to follow a more spiritual path, or to bring more spiritual awareness into their lives, they need to be creative. They need to let their imagination grow and expand; to seek out inspiration and insights and so nurture the creative urge.

It is also important to accept that as we open up to our creative impulses not every poem we write is necessarily the final word on the spiritual perspective of life, not every painting need be a window on to the divine. We wrestle to appreciate and translate the divine inspiration and understanding. Even Mongán, son of the sea god Mannanán mac Lir, admits that words fail him when he tries to describe the otherworld.

Not every one of us is as talented a poet as Taliesin or the legendary Amergin. Rather, if we can learn to be inspired by the nearness of the Celtic Angels, then through them the work we complete will be special for us. Over time others too may come to appreciate what we create, but the important point here is for us to enjoy the process of creation—whether it is painting, poetry, pottery or even gardening. In this chapter we will explore the ideas of why we create and we will start the process for ourselves. All this is a key part of our rediscovery of our spiritual needs and of course ultimately our Purpose of Life.

Celtic Angels Can Help You to Create

In truth we are all creative persons. Even something as basic as what we choose to wear is a creative process of sorts. After all, the style and colors we select are part of how we present ourselves to the world. How we display ornaments in our house, how we tend our garden, even how we cook food all reveal us as creative beings.

Just as any one of us can arrange cut flowers in a bowl, so we can write poetry or sing. Most of us can learn to play a musical instrument or paint a picture. However, we all use a battery of excuses that act as barriers to us becoming more creative. I was struck by this when I was giving a talk at Harrogate, a spa town in North Yorkshire. I was standing chatting to a group of people at the end of the talk and without any prompting on my part several of them commented that they were frustrated that they couldn't seem to find any time to do creative work. I was preparing to write this chapter and perhaps was more sensitive to these comments than usual. Or maybe my Anamcara was giving me a sign. Either way, I realized this in fact is true. Very few people seem to have the time to undertake these "hobbies."

When people retire it is amazing the numbers who take up painting, embroidery or any one of the creative arts. It is such a shame that they have had to wait until they retire before they do so. Wouldn't it be great if employers gave paid time off to allow us to pursue such pastimes? It has been argued that the creative revolution is the next big change to come to our post-industrial information-based economic society. Creative workers are innovative workers and innovation, of course, is the key to industrial success. Fulfilled workers are happy workers and also creative workers. For the industrialist it is a happy self-fulfilling circle.

Being creative is not only good for us workers, it is a crucial part of our spiritual development. It is, after all, a way in which we can express ourselves without constraint: we can write the most romantic stories or paint dramatic Gothic mountainscapes. The only thing that restricts us is our imagination. If you sit with a blank sheet of paper and create a whole countryside scene in pencil, where did that idea come from? What does it signify to you? Why did you do this and not something else? By considering these questions and working with our Anamcara, we are able to understand a lot more about ourselves and the demands and desires of our divine spark as we seek to fulfill our Purpose of Life.

However, not only do we have to overcome organizational problems such as lack of time. We also have to address our own reticence, our own insecurities that not only will people not be impressed by our creations, but those same creations may also reveal more of ourselves than we are willing to let people see.

I have been giving talks and running workshops now for several years. They started when I was told by my Celtic Angels that the time had come for me to go out and meet other people and tell them of my experiences. Although I had worked for years as a professor and lecturer at various universities, I found it very difficult to do this. This was because it was personal, it was part of me. And I was apprehensive about how people would react. In truth I had nothing to fear. In fact, the more I opened up, the more the people I was with would respond.

Even talking about Celtic Angels, I see the same. Only after I have described some of my encounters will others offer their experiences. So you may well come across this with your art as well. However, the choice is yours. You can be as open or as secretive about your creative works as you wish to be. You may paint sitting openly at the waterside or you may simply take a photo and paint from that, seeking to remember the emotional quality of that moment.

When you are working with your Celtic Angels another difficulty is trying to translate the emotions, ideas and visions that you create together into something physical. Sometimes our Celtic Angels give us the most amazing dreams. As a writer I often wake up and remember stunning plots and amazing dialogue. However when I begin to write it all down in my Dream Journal, somehow the depth and subtleties of the experience seem to defy me. I am left with just the bare bones. We do need to recognize that the words and tools we use are designed for this-world experiences. It is like the difference between a two-dimensional spade and a three-dimensional spade.

Recognizing this, we need to accept these limitations and then, even with our inferior tools, strive towards the creation of those special feelings. That is the challenge and the pain of creating. When you succeed it is also the joy and satisfaction of the process too!

YOU ARE CREATIVE!

Some people claim that they are simply not the creative type. They find excuses and justifications as to why they cannot create. They will even suggest that they lack inspiration. Of course none of this is true. It is only an excuse, and not even a good one. To reassure yourself, or to overcome severe cases of creative block, try this deceptively simple exercise.

Find a place to sit where you feel comfortable. Light a candle and do your invocation. Open your Angel Journal at a blank page and get some colored pencils. Now do the Angel Meditation.

As the Celtic Angels flow around you, feel their energy and serenity. Sense their eagerness and abilities and smile as you feel their love and care. Be aware of yourself floating there, free and contented.

Now, in your mind's eye, see three Celtic Angels come towards you. They are each holding a football, each of a different color. They let them go and they float in front of you.

Now open your eyes and immediately draw the three balls on the page of your journal.

Congratulations, you have done something creative!

Why do you suppose the Celtic Angels chose those colors for you? There has been a lot of work done on how different colors affect us: how they can stand for passive or active emotions; how they inspire images with us; and how they can aid our own healing processes.

Here, however, just consider what the colors suggest to you. Red, for example, might stand for anger or aggression. Why would you have been given that ball?

In your Angel Journal underneath the three balls write down what each color means to you and how you feel about it.

Congratulations, you have done something creative!

Perhaps a whole color can be reduced to one word. Yellow might stand for the sun which you enjoyed while on vacation. So "Hawaii" might be all you need to write. Now consider all that you have written and try to reduce it to three lines with three words on each. A poem!

Congratulations, you have done something creative!

Close your eyes again. Slowly feel yourself sinking into the soft, comfortable world of the Celtic Angels. Think of what you have done and feel a gentle sense of pride. But more than that, feel a connection with the divine that being creative has inspired in you.

Enjoy these sensations for a few moments and then, when you are ready, open your eyes and do your closing ceremony.

Getting Ready to Create

A key part of becoming a creative person is appreciating other people's creative work. This simple act can help us to feel the presence of the Celtic Angels as we experience sensations that are not based on the mundane material world. The emotions and ideas that a painting might engender in us are too complex to be defined in equations and glib one-word answers. And that is as it should be.

A trip to an art gallery is a good step here. With so many paintings, sculptures and other creative works in one place, it is impossible to interact with every piece of work. Look around and find a painting that you are drawn to. Try to work out why it appeals to you. Is it the style, the colors or maybe even the topic?

Take some time to investigate the painting properly. Every piece of art can be read on three levels. First of all there is the literal understanding. If it is a painting of a harbor, then, at this level, that is what the artist intended us to see and to understand. There is also the allegorical level. That is why did the painter choose to paint this harbor? And in this way? Why these colors? These shadows? A harbor might stand as a marketplace. Or maybe it should be seen as a safe haven in a storm. Perhaps storm clouds in the distance help to emphasize this. The scene then transforms from happy fishermen to anxious skippers awaiting the battering of the storm.

Third, there are the hidden meanings. These are revealed by the slightest hints in the painting. For example, there might be five boats, each in the colors of the ancient kingdoms of Ireland. The men on the boats might be a reference to the kings. Together in the harbor, but not really united. Write down all your thoughts in your journal. You might want to find out what you can about the artist; their own life may reveal more about the messages of the painting.

Now seek out a painting that you either feel no connection with or feel repelled by. Again, try to understand why. Write down all your thoughts in your journal.

You need to take some time to consult with your Anamcara and discuss what these attractions and dislikes tell you about your spiritual journey. This is an exercise that you can do with any form of art. It is fun and inspiring and helps us to appreciate that we are much more than just skin and bones. We have a soul that craves spiritual stimulation and appreciation of the creative arts.

Celtic Angels and Inspiration

Where does inspiration come from? What processes go on that we are not aware of before an idea emerges? When you work with the Celtic Angels, as you seek inspiration, your attention is diverted from your repetitive, relatively mundane, day-to-day life. Also you need to remember that the Celtic Angels are there to look out for you. They know that the more you work with your inspiration, the more you will fulfill your spiritual goals. They therefore want to help you. When they whisper ideas into your ear, they are seeking to guide and motivate you into working with particular images, ideas or even places.

When I started to write my first novel, *The T'sach*, I felt this process going on. As I researched the early years of the Munster Kings in southern Ireland, I was drawn again and again to the sparse information that there was on the Deisi, a tribal people in land to the east of the Munstermen in south-east Ireland. As the plot began to develop in my head, I was aware of Angel Whispers all around me and as I wrote the book I sometimes felt someone else was dictating the text. Later on, when I went back and read over the script, there were ideas expressed and descriptions of places that I had never thought of before. I was shocked, but also excited, to realize how much the Celtic Angels had helped me in the writing of it.

It is also quite exhilarating to realize the strength of the link we have between ourselves and our Celtic Angels as we create. That companionship can be very important. Normally, before I do any writing I meditate at my Angel Altar and do not close down until after I have finished writing.

I also keep a candle on my writing desk. When I light it, I ask for inspiration and guidance. When I am finished and blow it out, I thank the spirits for their help. These rituals are important because they alert us to the fact that we are about to create, to open ourselves up to the Celtic Angels and then, at the end, ask them to help us to close down and become more grounded again.

Creative Exercises

The purpose of these exercises is not to create masterpieces. You can show the finished treasures to others or keep them to yourself. The choice is yours. What you should never do is tear them up or destroy them. Every piece of art you create is a message from your Celtic Angels to you. Even if you do not understand the message, keep it, because one day you'll look back and recognize what is being said.

Almost certainly you will already be doing something creative in your life. But you should still do all the exercises here. Each art form uses different skills and can give you a different perspective. For example, I am a writer, but recently I have started writing a series of short stories inspired by some of my favorite songs and poems. Although I have only written a few so far, it is striking how different they are from the source. And yet by comparing and contrasting, the underlying message from both is highlighted quite clearly. I also enjoy playing music, though mostly I improvise and simply let the spirits flow!

PREPARATION

To begin these creative adventures first of all gather the materials you will need. Next, you need to modify your Angel Altar to help the inspiration to grow. Seek tall-reaching plants. If you would normally use a scented candle, try to increase the strength of the scent by switching to incense cones if you can. Try to take water from a sacred site or spot that you have visited recently and found conducive to creative thoughts. For fire burn a blue or aquamarine candle. For earth find a large quartz crystal ball if you can or as large a crystal as possible. Quartz crystal balls are magical items. Unlike lead crystal balls, which are clear, these ones are full of lines and shapes. You only have to glance at them and you can see the mist forming within. The shapes begin to move. It is a great tool for awakening the creative source.

Now, sitting in front of the Angel Altar, light your candle and incense, and, when you are ready, close your eyes and do the Angel Meditation. Take your time and enjoy the arrival of the angels.

With the Celtic Angels whirling around you, call on your Anamcara and feel them approach you. If you have artists or craftspeople among your ancestors, ask your Anamcara if you should call on them too.

When you are ready, pull up your roots and then open your eyes. Remember that you are still in close contact with your Celtic Angels so only work on your creative projects. Don't get distracted because you are not able at the present moment to engage with the ordinary world.

WRITING A SHORT STORY

Take a book. Open it at random and ask your Anamcara to look at the page and give you the number of a line. Count down that number of lines. Now ask for a number for the word along that line. Count along and write down that word.

Repeat this exercise until you have been given five words. The point of this exercise is for you to write a short story, say around 1,200 words, using all five words in the order in which they come. Close your eyes and once again feel yourself sinking back into that meditative calm.

When you have reached inner calm, offer up each of the words. See what images or ideas come to you.

Once you have some kind of idea for a story, sketch it out, first making sure you know how you are going to use the five words. When you have it clear in your own mind, write it out. Try not to revise it too often as that can mean your writing loses something of its spontaneity.

WRITING A POEM

While you can do this exercise with almost any object, why not begin by trying to write "An Ode to a Twig"? Go and find a twig in the woods. You will find this easier if you know what kind of tree it comes from, or, if you don't know the name, at least what it looks like.

As you do the Angel Meditation this time, hold the twig in your hand and as the Celtic Angels whirl about and your Anamcara approaches, consider in your mind's eye how the twig looks now. It may seem quite different.

Ask your Anamcara how they would describe it. Hold it out to the Celtic Angels and see if any of them takes an interest in it.

Now clear your mind and see what words and images drift in. Don't judge these ideas, simply try to remember them and as soon as you have finished your meditation write them all down in your journal. This is the raw material from which your poem will be drawn.

When you feel ready, do the Angel Meditation again. Now in the world of the Celtic Angels once more, try to compose a poem using as many of the words and ideas as you can remember. This is not easy as we no longer have great memory skills, but persevere.

When you have finished try to work out the three levels of meaning of what you have written and what the Celtic Angels are trying to teach you.

SINGING A SONG

The growing number of amateur choirs shows the great popularity of singing. Whether at church, in the stadium bleachers or at a concert, there is something special about singing with others. True as this is, the presence of a soloist electrifies the concert.

There is something so magical about one voice soaring high into the heavens. That voice can make us weep, laugh or cheer. In this exercise you are that soloist, singing on your own.

Ideally this exercise should be done in the open air. You should consult your Anamcara and decide where you want to go. Once you are there do your invocation and then the Angel Meditation.

When you are ready, open your eyes and look around. You will find that as you sing the tune you create and the words you use will change. Start, however, by noticing something you can see and then decide what is unusual about it. "I can see a mountain. It is like a pyramid." Take the last word of that line and just sing whatever comes into your mind. Don't even think about the tune. "Sandy and gray and distant in time."

This form of spontaneous singing is actually very easy, though you may not think it. The difficulty lies in remembering all the words as you create them, for once you are finished you will want to write down the words and tune so that you can refer back to them.

If you can write music, writing down the tune will be no problem. If, like most people, you can't write music, simply try to write the shape of the music. Start with a dot on the line. If the next note is a little higher, then place the next dot a little higher; if the next note is a lot higher, place the note much higher on the paper. You just need a prompt so that when you come back you can get the rough outline of the music. You will quickly remember.

Celtic poets and bards when they were composing would work forward line by line, constantly repeating until they were happy that they were word- and tone-perfect. That is what you have to do as well.

CREATING A PICTURE

Find a glossy magazine with lots of different kinds of photos in it. Then ask your Anamcara for ten page numbers. Tear these pages out and lay them side by side. See which images on each page draw your eye.

You are going to create a collage with one image from each page. First of all cut out the ten images and then see how you feel they should go together. Listen to the Angel Whispers as they tell you ways of linking these pictures. Once you have finished you will have not just ten separate photos but a new composite picture as well.

When you have completed these exercises, you need to close down as you would after a meditation. Take some time to reread what you have written in your journal or look again at the artwork. Attempt to understand what is being said here. Try to remember the subtle emotions you felt; how the ideas felt as they came to you and the different images and impressions that you were working with. Finally, judge how closely the work you have done compares to that larger whole.

Creativity is a powerful force for us to use as we develop our spiritual understandings. As we work with our Celtic Angels, it is as if we become merely the tools for our souls to communicate and teach themselves. The created artwork is the outward representation of this intense inner revelation. To be a part of this, and to recognize this, is a great gift.

As we work with our Anamcara we are seeking not necessarily to create great masterpieces or works that will be admired for hundreds of years; rather we are seeking to express our innermost thoughts and emotions. We are aiming to speak with the voice of our soul, our divine spark. And the reward for this is our own spiritual awareness and contentment. We are just so lucky that we can truly appreciate it.

SIXTEEN

Celtic Angels Can Help Us to Cope

Celtic Angels are with us all the time and by now you should be familiar with the sense of them always being around you. Equally, your Anamcara is there for you too. You should already feel comfortable with the idea of calling on them and feeling them appear at your side.

There are certain pivotal moments in your life when the presence of your Celtic Angel is a comfort and an additional resource to call on to see you through. In this chapter we look at how the Celts saw these rites of passage and how the Celtic Angels can smooth the transition for you.

Birth

Take a moment to think what happens when a baby is born. The baby was only conceived because a divine spark chose to allow itself to be trapped once again in the material world. In the womb an incredible biological machine is created, a machine with a spirit. When a baby is born all three parts are unfolding: the mind is becoming fully active, the body is becoming autonomous and the spirit is once again in the material world.

Because the spirit comes into the baby at the point of conception, its rest in the womb is a special time. If you are pregnant you need to be aware that the spirit is indeed at rest and you should try not to disturb it. You should be careful with meditation and other spiritual exercises during this time, perhaps restricting yourself to light breathing-focused meditations and visualizations.

You should also rejoice that your own Celtic Angels will be gathering to protect you and the baby. St. Columba's mother, when she was pregnant, was visited in her dreams by Celtic Angels who draped a cloak of many colors over her to keep her warm and protect her and her precious baby.

Traditionally, when babies were born in the Western Isles, the midwife passed them over the fire three times with words murmured to the fire god. And a gold or silver coin was added to the first water used to bathe the newly born for good luck. The midwife also gave a pre-baptism to prevent "no seed of fairy, no seed of the hosts of the air . . . lift[ing] away the happy little sleeper." Clearly a version of a much older ceremony, this practice shows the Celts believed that the soul was not yet a permanent fixture within the body and could be easily removed. Souls were only fixed once they were connected with the physical body and the mind through the naming ceremony or baptism. Fortunately, the midwife's pre-baptism was recognized by the Church in the islands, for no unbaptized babies could be buried in consecrated ground.

When a baby is born you should welcome not just the baby but also their divine spark and the Celtic Angels who will have gathered around them. For, from the earliest moments, Celtic Angels will gather, attracted both by the excitement and magic of a new baby but also by the ancient divine spark residing within.

How aware the divine spark is at this time is unknown; it may well be almost suffocated by the rapid development of the new body. Many young children, however, have a vivid understanding of the otherworlds that we, as adults, can only marvel at. It is a tragedy that as we grow up we are encouraged to discard such an awareness until eventually we forget how to connect to the spiritual realms altogether.

One story I heard, which I suspect may be an urban myth, was that of a small girl who was deeply jealous as her mother grew heavily pregnant and, when her father explained what was happening, turned hostile towards the new baby. After the baby was born, the parents were very nervous about leaving the young girl with the baby unattended. However, one night they heard, over the intercom set up in the bedroom where the baby was sleeping, the voice of the little girl talking to the baby and saying, "Tell me again what it's like with the angels. I seem to keep forgetting as I grow older!"

Whether the story is true or not, the sentiment is valid. As we grow and discover more of the material world, its vastness and richness overwhelm us and our ability to focus on spiritual matters lessens.

It is therefore important that children are encouraged to be aware of the spiritual realms and their Celtic Angels from as early an age as possible. If you talk to them about your own experiences, that will show them that what they are aware of is not fancy or childish illusions, but real. And, following your lead, they will embrace this awareness and not feel embarrassed or ashamed.

Children also have an almost unending desire to be creative. There is an adage that states that in creativity quantity means quality; in other words the more solutions to a problem you can think of, the more creative you are being. Sad, then, that one study showed that, given most problems, adults will come up with on average six possible solutions while a child will come up with sixty.

You should encourage children's creativity in all its forms. Get them to paint pictures of their Celtic Angels or write letters to them. When you visit sacred sites make sure that they give gifts to the spirits of the site. The more you encourage them, the more they will respond. And if you start from an early enough age, they will simply accept all this as normal.

Of course not all babies grow up into adulthood and one of the most common questions people ask is how can any god allow horrible things to happen to small innocent children. And it is a good question—if you accept that the god is omnipotent. As we have shown here the Godhead is a benign force that can do nothing except exist.

Celts worshiped local gods and goddesses but seem to have accepted that their powers were limited. We all, in the end, die. It just seems so tragic when the life lost is a young one.

Celtic Angels are there with every one of us. However, even their powers to intervene are limited. They might warn against going swimming in the raging river, but if the boy refuses to hear they cannot physically stop the child from entering the water.

Anamcara can sometimes materialize in our realms but that is rare, and while the Bible and Celtic saint hagiographies are full of stories of angels aiding and assisting humans in need, the truth is that such interventions are only occasional. It may be that the effort of actually materializing on this earth is so difficult that only a few Celtic Angels have mastered it. It may be that the danger is so sudden, like being struck with lightning, that the angels have no time to act.

When babies are born only to die a few painful days later, it is again difficult to accept that any divine being would allow such a thing. All that can be said is that the spirit chose to be born there. Perhaps the lesson it had to learn was related to pain. Maybe it wished to help the souls of the parents understand something related to the whole experience. We can only trust that no baby dies in vain; that we all learn something special and have cherished memories to comfort us in our own lives.

Such tragedy does occur, however, and it shows the rest of us how lucky we are. And how we should celebrate each moment of life, for life truly is a sacred gift.

Falling in Love

One of the most precious experiences any of us can have is falling in love and even more so when that feeling is reciprocated. That sense of being special, being appreciated and being adored is something we don't get enough of. Yet our relationship with our Celtic Angels is very similar. As you get used to being with your Anamcara, if you cannot sense them around you, you begin to feel bereft, abandoned. Of course they *are* there, it is us who have tuned out momentarily, no doubt distracted by other things.

Celtic magic is full of spells for finding your true love and for winning their heart. However, what we are really talking about is the bonding of two spirits. We do not talk about being *deeply* in love for no reason. Physical attraction is fine and dandy to begin with but if your souls don't connect then there is only shallow physical fulfillment, and no matter how fine the food we all soon tire of haute cuisine.

We all meet hundreds if not thousands of people in our daily life yet only a few become acquaintances, even fewer become friends and almost uniquely do we actually fall in love with someone. Even more amazing is that while we may love our closest friends, we are not in love with them. What is it that marks out some people to be our friends and the very occasional other to be someone we fall in love with?

When we fall in love our Celtic Angels are involved too. They link on the spiritual plane just as we link on the physical one. Whether they initiate the process or react to our maneuver is hard to say. What is important is that for the relationship to develop into mutual love then the Celtic Angels must be involved.

To be in love is a special spiritual experience. Now there is someone else who is not originally part of the family background who cares about us and is there for us. It is a totally empowering experience.

We can experience something very similar with our Anamcara. Again, this is the kind of emotional and spiritual relationship that reassures and nurtures us. Your Anamcara is always there, always for you and loves you in a powerful and delightful way. And when we return that love, when we value our relationship with our Anamcara and work closely with them, then we complete the cycle. We create together a powerful and energizing relationship. To love and be loved, what could be better?

Ill Health

If we are working with our Celtic Angels, seeking to follow a compassionate spiritual life, many people feel that we shouldn't experience any ill health or pain. The truth is that our body is just like a car and no matter how much we look after it, it will eventually deteriorate and decay. Pain and ill health are the results.

However, not all of this is bad news. By working with our Celtic Angels we can be shown how many of our ailments are self-imposed. American author and doctor Bernie Segal, from his days working in the hospital wards, tells a story of a woman who was brought in suffering from a form of terminal cancer. Her overbearing and bullying husband then died suddenly. Although the family tried to shield her from the news, she found out and from that moment began to improve, eventually making a full recovery. She had been in a situation where she had no life of her own and had simply given up. The death of her husband meant that she now had something to live for.

This might seem fantastic or just simplistic, but we all accept the idea of psychosomatic illness where we make ourselves ill. I used to work as a freelance teacher and I only got paid for the work I did. If I could not teach a class, even if I was ill, I would not get paid. Needless to say I was almost never ill. Come the end of the semester, however, and I would almost always contract a cold or sore throat. I was simply not letting myself become ill until I could afford to.

The last time I had to take to my bed with a cold, it was only a few days after I had been thinking of how hard I had been working and how I could do with a few days in bed. Be careful what you wish for!

If these principles happen in such a way then why not with more complex diseases as well? Many holistic healers, when you consult them, will quiz you more on your lifestyle, hopes and ambitions than the actual malady, because they recognize how powerful we are at controlling our own health. Of course this is not a totally comforting thought. To realize that we may be the cause of our own illness is daunting and even frightening. However, if we accept that our own state of mind may be a contributing factor, then clearly we need to do something about it.

The Celtic Angels, as beings who have left a corporeal existence behind, might be expected to be disinterested or even hostile to our problems. But that could not be further from the truth. Work with your Anamcara to find out why you are suffering from illness and how to change your attitude to help your body to mend.

It might even be possible to learn from our illness. While one Irish healer I know was creating a series of essences, she manifested every major illness she was constructing a cure for.

It was a terrifying time for her, but also a humbling one as she learned about the emotional and psychological aspects of an illness, not just its physical manifestation.

Of course prevention is better than cure. We have little idea what kind of medical knowledge the ancient Celts had. The Druids, followed by the Celtic saints, would certainly have had a good knowledge of herbs and other natural cures. Every family would probably also have had a Wise Woman who would oversee the well-being of the clachan. Generally, however, the health of the people was probably similar to today.

Life was certainly harder then and there would have been no need for gyms and exercise classes. Everyone would have been involved in some sort of manual labor. And as we have seen with St. Senan, Celtic Angels could help with that.

Climbing the sacred mountain of Croagh Patrick in western Ireland, I was shocked how steep and rough the missionary trail was. I had expected a much more leisurely stroll than the hard, steep climb that faced me. There was a point where I had to stop every hundred steps to catch my breath, then it was fifty and then twenty-five. My rucksack seemed to be getting heavier and heavier and, as I looked ahead of me, there seemed no respite as the path slowly wound around the side of the hill. It was only sheer dogged determination that kept me going.

My Anamcara was fine, of course, pointing out interesting shapes and colors in the heather and bracken. Eventually I felt I could go no further. Each step was a slow, hard grind. I asked my Anamcara for help. He smiled and came up behind and I felt him pushing my rucksack and giving me just that little bit of extra power I needed. He did it only for about thirty steps or so, but it was enough and I slowly plodded on, eventually reaching the top!

Research has shown that in the eighteenth century, if you survived the first five years of your life, survived childbirth and didn't die in battle, then you had a very good chance of living well into your seventies. This may seem unbelievable to us nowadays, as we are conditioned to thinking of people prior to the twentieth century leading short, brutal lives. Yet when we look at the lives of the Celtic saints, where we can be fairly certain of the birth and death years, it is clear that many of them lived well into old age. St. Adomnán was eighty when he died in A.D. 704, St. Columba seventy-six, St. Samson of Cornwall seventy-five and St. David was over ninety. And these men were by no means exceptional.

As spirits trapped in the material world it is our duty to keep our bodies in as good a shape as possible. After all, we want to make sure that we learn the lessons we intended to in this lifetime. It may be that some of us need as much time as possible. It is also true that the different ages of our life see us operate in different ways. While as children we rush everywhere and demand instant gratification, as more mature people we are content to appreciate more and do less. That is the natural rhythm of life and we should not fight it, but rather we should revel in it.

CELTIC ANGELS AND THE RHYTHM OF LIFE

This meditation works best if you can be in a natural forest. If you cannot visit such a place, you can of course do this in your own home but try to sense how it would feel out among the trees.

In the forest wander about until you find a place where you feel comfortable. To stand beside an ancient oak or yew and sense its age and serenity is an extremely moving spiritual experience in itself. Try, if you can, to feel the spirits draped all over the tree, sense the quiet, contented dreaming of the beings of this place and seek to bring that sense of acceptance into your own life.

When you are ready, make your invocation, close your eyes and then do the Angel Meditation. As you stand there surrounded by trees, feel the tranquil movement of your own Celtic Angels and then sense your Anamcara standing beside you.

Focus in and become aware of your own being inside your body. Feel the solid walls of your body holding you back. Feel their rigidity and permanence. However, such a wall cannot stop you! Simply slip down the roots from the soles of your feet into the ground and then up to stand beside your own body. This may sound difficult but I found I could master this exercise in only a few attempts.

In one simple fluid movement you are free! Your Anamcara will come to join you. Smile at each other and then look around you. Here, in the woods, you will meet trees in all stages of life from the young shoots just peeking out from the ground through the shriveled remains of last year's leaves to willowy adolescents and then trees in their full maturity, resplendent in their stature and vigor. Beside them will be older trees covered in lichen and ivy and then the skeletons of trees long dead and slowly decaying back into the soil.

It is a beautiful, inevitable circle. Take some time to be with each age of tree. Flow along and seek out the youngest of the young. Feel their uncertainty and hesitancy. Stop and reassure them. Sense the excitement and energy of the adolescent trees as they reach for the sky, sheltered by their elders, yet determined to succeed and one day become a great tree themselves.

Bow to the great masters of the forest. Seek out the silver birch, queen of the woods and the ancient oaks, the kings. Feel their mass and certainty. Touch their trunks and feel the solid acceptance of life. Let your fingers trace the complex patterns in the bark as you slowly become aware of the trunk swaying slightly in the wind.

The more elderly trees are slumbering in the gentle sun. They have left the energy and sense of self behind. They are content simply to be. They are resting and happy to do so, for there is little that is new to them and they accept that with grace and perhaps even a sense of relief.

Finally there are the trees that have died. There is a sadness there, a lack of spirit, for that has since departed. But as you look closer you see that a myriad of other creatures have made the tree their home, from birds and squirrels to beetles and other insects boring into the trunk. Life goes on.

Each stage of life has its beauties. Each stage of life is to be enjoyed and appreciated. And we need to understand that each stage of life has its lessons for us to learn and accept.

As you flow back through the forest with your Anamcara, think about these matters and send love and care to all the trees you meet. Listen to your Anamcara as they talk to you and try to comprehend the teaching they offer.

Now you have returned to where you started. Feel your awareness return into your body. Feel once again your body's walls around you. And when you are ready open your eyes. Make the sign for closure and then take a few minutes simply to become familiar again with where you are.

Death

What happens when you die is a question that has fascinated the human race since the very beginning of time. For the Celts, death is not the end, it is merely an interlude and a change of mode of existence.

Until the last century there was belief in many Celtic households that on Halloween, when the veil between the worlds was at its thinnest, the dead would come back to visit their living relatives.

The Celts knew that when you die something that was you remains, for they were able to access that. The divine spark that resides within is of course liberated and will be greeted by your Anamcara as spirit to spirit. They will then guide it on to the next rebirth and they may well stay with it for another lifetime.

So death can be seen in many ways as the beginning of a new existence as well as the end of the current one. This is something that we should celebrate. It is ultimately a step forward to the Godhead.

As we prepare ourselves for death, whether through old age or disease, our Celtic Angels can help us. Of course it is only natural that death frightens us, for it is the great unknown.

In some ways this is a true test of our spirituality. Do we really believe this? Or are we merely playing at being spiritual?

This is a challenge that only you can answer. If, like me, you have experienced meetings with the angels, if they have demonstrated time after time after time that they exist and are real, what is there to fear about death?

Take some time to think on this. What do you fear about death?

For me it is the fear of pain. Yet I know that in the modern world any pain will be transitory and will only make the ultimate release all the sweeter. Yet I am content to admit my fear.

The Celtic Angels are our proof that there is life after death, that our soul will move on. After all, at one time they too walked the earth as humans and one day we too will be angels. It is as simple as that!

Appreciating Coincidence

When you walk your spiritual path, you will notice that more and more coincidences seem to occur. This is not your imagination, it really is happening. It is because as you work with the flow of spiritual energy that is all around us, as we use our intuition and listen to the Angel Whispers, things that are meant to happen do happen. We think of people we have not seen for a long time and then we meet them in the street; we meet strangers and realize that we know many of the same people or share common hobbies. These life-affirming moments reassure us that we are walking the right path and are fitting into a greater spiritual pattern.

I was giving a talk in London and afterward a man came up and asked about St. Kessog of Luss, a saint whom I work with a lot. It turned out that the day before he had been in North Kessock, a town north of Inverness named after the saint and had also driven through Luss on Loch Lomond-side. This experience of course made my talk more vibrant and relevant to him and reaffirmed my own belief in the work I do. I see this sort of thing all the time, and it enriches my life.

Take some time now to write down in your Angel Journal all the coincidences that you have experienced recently. Try to remember how they came about. Did the angels whisper to you to take an earlier lunch and so you met a long-lost friend on the street? Did you feel the urge to call your sister just before she called you? Try to be constantly aware of affirming events and signs that reassure you that the Celtic Angels are really there. Keep doing this until you can look in the mirror and admit that you *know* the Celtic Angels are with you.

To know absolutely that the Celtic Angels are there is not easy, especially when you link it with the idea of your own mortality. But once you accept the Celtic Angels, a huge weight is lifted from you and you can accept that death, when it comes, is merely another stage on the road to the Godhead.

As spirits in the material world, we are here because we have lessons we have to learn. Death sometimes sneaks up on us unawares: we might be knocked down by a bus or suddenly discover we have a terminal disease. How terrible it would be in those last few moments to realize the importance of all the things we had always felt a longing to do but had put off because we were too busy with our day-to-day life.

Our Celtic Angels are there to remind us of that. We sense their freedom, their contentment and their peace. That is what we crave and desire. It would be sad if our epitaph was only that he was a hard-working, dedicated insurance application-form processor.

As we die or even as our divine spark leaves this life to move on, we want to be content and satisfied. We want the divine spark to have learned its lessons and to be fulfilled and ready for the next step, not full of regrets and the realization that it is going to have to go back and do it all again.

To ensure success, we need to listen constantly to our Celtic Angels and our Anamcara in particular. They can teach and guide us. They can show us how we can succeed and encourage us as we stumble forward. In the penultimate chapter we go on to consider this further and show how we can incorporate spirituality and the Celtic Angels in particular into every aspect of our day-to-day lives. And by so doing succeed in our Purpose of Life.

SEVENTEEN

Everyday Life with the Celtic Angels

The steam room of the local health club might seem an odd place to talk with your Anamcara. But there I was, sitting in a daydream, the heat softening my thoughts and lulling me into a stupor, when I became aware of his presence at my side. His mere appearance, of course, was enough for my heat-befuddled brain to start becoming aware of more spiritual matters.

No matter how often we remind ourselves, it remains difficult to grasp that our Celtic Angels are with us all the time, day and night. We can appreciate them and talk with them at any time. In this chapter we try to make sense of this and show how, with some simple exercises, we can be constantly aware of their presence.

Are Celtic Angels Really with Us All the Time?

The simple answer to this question is yes, they are. A more interesting question is, what are they doing while they are with us? We have to appreciate, first of all, that spirits are not the same as us. While they have an awareness that we can communicate with, they do not have bodies as we understand the term. To make it easy for us they appear with a body, but that is just a facade, an exterior. We can only imagine what it must be like to exist without a body; we have no experience to which we can liken it.

However, it may well be that spirits, although they are with us, are also elsewhere. Perhaps they are able to focus on several different aspects at once: one part of them is with me, one is watching somewhere else and a third part is contemplating the divine.

I have certainly found over time that there seem to be occasions when my Anamcara seems more present, more "here." While that may be, it is also possible simply that I am able to perceive him more clearly at some times rather than others. But this teaching seems true to me, though my Anamcara has been silent on the matter.

The anonymous Celtic Angels who whirl around are attracted by the spiritual energy that we give off. Some of these angels will stay with you for long periods of time to the point where you may begin to recognize some of them. Other angels come and go; they may even appear only because they have a specific message for you or task for you to complete.

Your Anamcara, however, has made a commitment to you and will always be there for you. But they are not of this world and, as we have already noted, their ability to change events here to make our life better, safer or more fulfilling is limited. Basically, if we ignore our Anamcara's suggestion to walk home a different way from work, we may miss the chance to meet someone or see something that might change our life for the better. Our Anamcara cannot force us to walk that way, they can only suggest. Ultimately it is up to us!

Celtic Angels in the Home

You will already have made changes in your home. You will have an Angel Altar that you tend on a regular basis and use in your Angel Meditations. Be aware that you may wish to change the site of your altar from time to time. Always be conscious of how comfortable it feels as you prepare to meditate. Your Anamcara may suggest to you changes that you should make, and you should follow those ideas wherever possible. Particular colors may be more conducive than others. Blue and white are two colors that are traditionally associated not only with angels, but spirits in general.

You may well have other angel products around you. Friends often respond to our interest in matters angelic come birthdays and Christmas, and slowly statues, prints, candle holders and all sorts of other angel-inspired goods begin to appear in the home. Try to acknowledge each of these items and what their symbolism means every day. It is too easy for these objects to merge into the background, so why not make a point of moving some of them around once a week. Moving these objects not only draws your attention to them when you enter a room, it also energizes the spirits that are associated with them and so makes them seem to glow and so, of course, draws your attention to them all the more. It is well known in the book-selling trade that if you have books that are not selling well, they will almost certainly sell within a couple of days if you handle them, give them a dust or simply flick through them: where your attention goes, energy flows!

Your daily routine should also incorporate angel work. In the morning after you have completed your Dream Journal, you should get up and spend some time at your Angel Altar or at least engaged in some kind of angel work. You could reread old Angel Journals. This is a great way to start the day because when you go back and reread what you were up to several years ago or even just a year ago, you realize how much you have progressed spiritually in that time.

Alternatively, you might buy a book of affirmations and take some time to contemplate the one you have picked for today. Affirmations are short verses or prose selected because of their upbeat, positive style. Their job is to inspire you. Some of these books allocate one for each day and you can follow them if you want, although I always prefer to ask my Anamcara. What to do is open the book without looking at the page and show it to them. They will let you know, yes or no. Nowadays you can even get some affirmation books themed on angels.

You should set aside some time each day for meditation. This may be in the morning when you are still relatively calm and unburdened after your night's sleep. It need not take a long time; normally ten to fifteen minutes is sufficient. From time to time you may want to enjoy a much deeper, longer meditation, but you should not expect to do that every day.

If you have a garden, then take time to create an angel-friendly space. Seek out the parts of the garden that seem most appropriate and cultivate areas of deep foliage where you can imagine nature sprites and other magical creatures could gather. This can be fun and helps you to see your garden as a more magical place.

Next you want to set up an Angel Altar somewhere in the garden, ideally in a secluded spot where you are not watched. If that is not possible, simply find the place where you feel most comfortable, preferably where you can face towards the east. Items for an outdoor altar need to be more robust than for an indoor one. But you can spread them out around you which helps to create even more of an impression of stepping into your own special world. You can buy stone angels in most garden centers these days, although they tend to be a bit cutsy. But you never know, you might be lucky and find one you like.

Nature, of course, is already present. For the five elements, an outdoor waterfall or fountain is possible, and are a lot cheaper than they used to be. Again, earth is no problem! For air, why not get a weather vane or small toy windmill? Even on the calmest of days they are there to remind you of the air. Finally, for fire you will need a storm lantern or similar device to prevent the candle flame from blowing out. Another possibility is a chiminea. These are like large versions of aromatherapy burners, where effectively you have a portable fireplace. They can be very small or large enough to use as a barbecue. Not only can you burn wood in these, you can add scents, pine cones for example, to enhance the special nature of the occasion.

In terms of plants and trees, angels are most associated with ash and elderflower, though beware that the first grows to a huge height, and the second grows everywhere! Ash is the tree associated with inner and outer meditation, which grows up into the heavens and down deep into the earth. Elderflower is associated with the fairies, and even today I know traditional tree workers who will not chop it down.

Think of other opportunities to reaffirm your awareness of the Celtic Angels. For example, you might find an attractive angel to have on your car dashboard; there are some amusing angel-themed car bumper stickers you can buy as well.

In the house, seek your Celtic Angels' blessing before you do any cooking, cleaning or decorating. Before you start cooking, for example, feel your Anamcara beside you and try to involve them in what you are doing. Talk to them, if that feels comfortable. Try to imbue all you do with a loving spirituality that hopefully will be appreciated by those who are going to eat the food—even if that is only you. Value yourself; after all, you deserve care, attention and pampering as much as anyone else.

Celtic Angels at Work

Try using the same principles at work. If you have a desk, why not create a sacred space there, with a plant, a small bowl of water and a scented nightlight. Place some quartz pebbles around the plant to stand for angel influence if you feel unable to have an angel statue. If you do this, it means that every time you sit at your desk you are entering your own special world, a world of angels.

You should also be aware of others at your work. Look for signs that they too are interested in working with the angels. They might wear an angel brooch, or a tie pin with an angel on it. They may have a picture of an angel on their desk or in their locker or it may just be something that they say. Remember, most people do believe in angels, and while they might not have the same intense relationship with the Celtic Angels as you have, nonetheless they have ideas and experiences to share. As I know only too well, the more people you talk to about your spiritual work, the more you learn yourself.

Don't forget that working with the Celtic Angels is about trying to follow a compassionate life every minute of the day. In a perfect world, we would consider every action and ask, is this the most compassionate way I can deal with this situation? In reality of course we conduct most of our work by habit. "This is the way we do what we do." Why not take some time and consider if it is the most compassionate way of behaving? I had a friend who was a credit controller. She worked for a large company and her job was mainly to call people and hassle them for money for outstanding invoices. Of course this was money that was due to the company; these people had entered into some kind of agreement, the bottom line of which was that they had agreed to pay the money by a certain date. My friend found that she was much more effective if she was pleasant and conciliatory on the phone. Instead of demanding the money "or else," she would be sympathetic and polite, merely asking if they could make some contribution towards the amount outstanding and agree on terms to pay all that was due. In her own way she was being compassionate and walking the path of the Celtic Angels.

Celtic Angels can even help you in your work itself. One woman told me how, at work, she kept being told by her Celtic Angels to check one supplier. She couldn't understand because she had e-mailed the order herself and they had never let her down before. But eventually, after several days of nagging, she did phone to check that the delivery would be there at the appropriate time and discovered the company had changed all their e-mail addresses and the old ones were not being forwarded, so they had no record of the order. Fortunately there was still enough time to rectify the situation. But as the woman said, "How spooky is that?" Well, not spooky at all. Her Anamcara was obviously aware of the situation and was seeking to avert a major crisis which would have upset the woman and interfered with her spiritual work.

As in the home, there are many tasks that we do at work where you may feel it is appropriate for you to ask for your Celtic Angels' blessings. I do this all the time. We sell my books and CDs on the Internet and every package is appreciated by my partner and me before it is sent out. We thank our Celtic Angels for what is happening to us and hope that the book and CD help the people who are about to receive them. Even in bookstores, when I see my book I make a point of handling each one and seeking a blessing for it and the person who will eventually buy it. Apart from anything else it is a comforting thing to do. It makes me feel better and hopefully the future reader does as well.

The most obvious seeking of blessing is when we travel. For fishermen and many others, being away from home is a fact of working life. In Scotland, with its strong fishing traditions, St. Michael's feast day on September 29 was the main festival day of the year. St. Michael is a Christianizing of Mannanán mac Lir, probably the best known of the Celtic gods of the sea. Even today, if you find any old churches dedicated to St. Michael they are almost without exception by the sea or high on a hill, for Mannanán mac Lir was also the god of messages.

CREATING A CELTIC BLESSING

Find somewhere you feel comfortable and do your invocation. Have your Angel Journal with you. Do the Angel Meditation and, when you are ready, move on to meet your Anamcara. We are going to create a Celtic blessing for travel, but you can use this approach to devise a blessing for any occasion you choose. Talk with your Anamcara about how you feel about travel. Do you get apprehensive before a long journey? Are you expected to organize everyone else? Or do you just throw everything together at the last moment? Think of the good emotions as well, the excitement, expectation and thrill of going somewhere new. The stimulation of meeting new people and seeing new landscapes can also make all the inconvenience of travel worth while.

Ask your Anamcara to help you to compose a blessing to use before you travel. A blessing, a bit like a spell, is designed to focus your thoughts and energies on the task ahead. However it is also creative, like poetry. Every word needs to have power and you are trying to take all the positive emotions about traveling and distill them down to a few words. Your Celtic Angels will help you to do this.

Slowly a blessing will emerge. Taste each word as it appears. Consider it and accept or reject it as you feel appropriate. You may need several sittings before you have a blessing that encompasses all the emotions and positive energy you want.

When you are finished, remember to thank your Anamcara and Celtic Angels for their support and then to close down. Make sure you write down your blessing in your Angel Journal. You might also want to make copies of it to carry with you. Take some time to consider what the blessing actually means. Try to sense how you will feel when you say it and how giving this blessing will change your attitude.

An example of a blessing for traveling is:

> May Brigit and Mary and Michael,
> Shield you on sea and on land,
> Each step and each path you travel.

This would almost certainly be a pre-Christian blessing that had been adjusted, the original verse being dedicated to Brigid and Mannanán mac Lir.

Of course once you have created a blessing for travel, you can repeat the exercise for anything else you want the Celtic Angels to help with. You can ask for their specific help, or their help in gathering other sources of aid. An example of an ancient Scottish one is:

> Power of the raven be thine,
> Power of the eagle be thine,
> Power of the Fiann.
>
> Power of the storm be thine,
> Power of the moon be thine,
> Power of the Sun.

With such a blessing you are wishing them the protection of the spirit realms, the power of the eagle and the ability to succeed. You are wishing them energy, insight and power over emotions and a general wish for good luck and success. Truly a powerful blessing.

Celtic Angels at Play

Even when you are enjoying yourself, the Celtic Angels and your Anamcara are there for you. If you play sports, try to sense them standing watching you. I used to play squash, and the first-floor viewing gallery was behind me. It was only too easy to feel my Anamcara standing there critically watching me play.

As you go about your day-to-day life, from time to time stop and see if you can sense where your Anamcara is. On the autumn equinox this year the weather was dry but very windy; too windy for the normal bonfire. My partner and I decided to go out under the trees in our garden and light our small chiminea instead. We have small resin-soaked fire blocks that light quickly and give off a strong, rich aroma. To these I added tiny twigs of elder, the tree that connects the old with the new, the past with the future. And as we sat there sheltered from the wind with the dark trees swaying above it was a beautiful, intimate moment.

In the silence my thoughts turned to my Anamcara and I cast about trying to find him. Once you've worked with your Anamcara long enough, you learn to identify their essence. So I can easily send out my own awareness in all directions seeking him. Often we will not communicate, but I like to know where he is, especially at special times like this. He was there, of course, standing beside a young ash tree. Probably, like me, he was enjoying the moment looking up at the clear night sky, tracing the flow of the Milky Way through the branches of the tree.

You can also create small ceremonies to remind yourself of the presence of your Anamcara and the other Celtic Angels. It doesn't have to be as obvious as having an extra chair at the table. One woman told me how her husband, brought up on one of the Western Hebrides, still leaves a small piece of food on his plate "for the angels." So whenever you eat or drink something, leave an angel's share. It can be the smallest of small amounts; after all the angels aren't actually going to eat it. But the act of doing this reminds us of the Celtic Angels who are all around us and of our desire to share our lives with them. Even if you forget, you can apologize and again you are remembering the angels.

Other similar ideas include always having a vase of cut flowers for the angels to appreciate, though they might prefer a living plant. If you have a garden, why not create a flowerbed for the glory of the Celtic Angels. See if you can discover which flowers or plants they are attracted to more than others. I have noticed that lavender seems to draw them. Otherwise just choose your own favorite blooms.

No Task Too Small . . .

As we saw in Chapter 5, no task is too small for the Celtic Angels. It can, after all, be the small things that upset and distress us more than the major world crises. While wars may rage, it is the loss of our grandmother's wedding ring that can reduce us to tears. It is not surprising then that the Celtic Angels will act as messengers, couriers or even lookouts for us.

FINDING A PARKING SPACE

This exercise is fun because it uses our intuition fused with Angelic Whispers. The idea here is that our Celtic Angels can see more than we can, they can flow over the land and report back. So if you are in a busy town center or large crowded parking lot, why not ask your angels to help you to find a parking space?

To some this may seem a frivolous use of angels. But it does serve a very important role: it confirms to us that we are indeed working with the angels. As you approach the parking area, ask your Celtic Angels out loud for help. Explain to them why, from a spiritual point of view, it would be good to find a space quickly, and then wait to be inspired. Proceed the way you feel drawn and you should find a space.

However, the more connected you are to your Celtic Angels the more you will come to realize that while you feel you are acting in an intuitive way, in fact you are following their advice. For the more you are open to angelic influence, the more you will listen to the Angel Whispers. And of course that opens you up to an appreciation of the magical world that surrounds us all.

For the Celts this magical world was part of their everyday life. As we have seen they asked the angels and gods for favors and blessings with almost every action they took. Every aspect of their life saw them working with the Celtic Angels. How wonderful it is to share the responsibilities and chores of day-to-day life. How inspiring it is to have someone there for you, and only you, all the time, and how great it is to know that, with the help of the Celtic Angels and your Anamcara, you will succeed.

Together you are a fabulous team! In the next, and final, chapter we show how you can fulfill your life's potential. You will work together to try to understand the reason why you are here today and the lessons you need to learn. With the support you have, how can you fail?

EIGHTEEN

Discovering Your Purpose of Life

This final chapter is really one long exercise. An exercise that will last all your life. An exercise that is the most important spiritual work you will do. You might want to start a new Purpose of Life Journal for this. Your aim at the end is to understand better why your life has evolved the way it has and what lessons you still need to learn in order, in the next lifetime, to proceed onwards towards the Godhead.

I'm sure you must have done this: you look back over your life and wonder how you ended up where you are now. I certainly do. My life, it seems, is a mystery: a confusion of opportunity, luck and occasional bouts of steely determination. And yet when I really consider all the steps in my life, there is a logic, a path that leads inexorably to where I am now. Imperfect as this place may be, it is nonetheless special to me and I am content.

I like to tell the story of when I decided, about ten years ago, that I wanted to go back to college and study for my doctorate. Even as I was making the decision, I knew it was wrong. I suspect my partner knew this as well but he kept quiet and has so far managed to resist saying, "I told you so."

Every grant I applied for was refused. Even the research proceeded a lot less smoothly than it should have. I felt as if I were wading through molasses. Eventually my supervisor fell ill and I could not continue any further. My relief was almost tangible.

It is so strange that even when we know we are making a mistake, we proceed anyway. Why can't we just admit it?

As soon as I stopped the research and returned to working full-time for my own New Age events company, Body & Soul, good things began to happen. The business began to grow, I started to write fiction again and I met some inspiring people who were to encourage me to write *Walking the Mist*.

One of the saddest things I hear is when people talk about lost years. Only today a woman who runs a store near our own was bemoaning that she had wasted the last twenty years. Now, as she was learning more about herself and her life, she wished this had all happened years before. Of course, I argued, it couldn't have because she was not in a place where such self-analysis would have worked for her. Grudgingly she agreed, but I sensed she wasn't totally convinced.

In my own case we moved out of Edinburgh in 1989, to the country to allow me to find inspiration and space to write. Yet it took some eleven years before I was able to dedicate myself seriously to the writing craft and another four years before *Walking the Mist* was published. Like my friend I am prone to think of those fifteen years, that intervening period, as wasted time. More than once I've beaten myself mentally for the lack of discipline, inspiration and commitment to my writing during those years.

Yet the truth is that if I hadn't done the teaching I did, attended the different types of classes, met the spiritual teachers and students that have made the years with Body & Soul so rewarding, then I could never have written *Walking the Mist*. Even the times sitting on top of a hill, meditating by the sea or wandering in a forest of young oak trees, these times too are part of who I am now.

So take some time and sit and appreciate all those occasions, events and people in your life that have made you who you are now. It is both humbling and inspiring to realize that we are all unique human beings. We are all special. And we are all on a journey: a one-way ticket to spiritual awareness and the Godhead.

The Spiritual Path

As we have already noted, we all carry within us a divine spark which longs to return to the Godhead. This life will eventually be a crucial step in helping it to leave the earth plane behind and move forward until one day it can rejoin the Godhead. When the divine spark chose to be born in us, there was an expectation of how our life would develop. Of course there are a million and one ways in which our life can be changed by others, and few of those changes would have been predicted. For example, your parents might win the lottery. That could change your life completely.

Nonetheless the underlying flow of your life is set when you are born and, like deep currents in a river, it is that flow, that path that we need to discover and accept if we want to follow our spiritual path and so learn our lessons.

This path of spiritual learning is like a track that winds through the woods. When we stay on the path, it is easier to move forward. If we are distracted and wander off the path, progress becomes much more difficult. If someone blocks our path with a fallen tree, it is often difficult to find a way around and back on to the path. Instead we stumble over roots and get caught in bramble bushes and may even lose our way altogether. Sometimes we can see the path and work back towards it; other times, like me and my Ph.D., we simply have to retreat back the way we came, until we find where we left the path.

The Purpose of Life

In this chapter we are going to look at how we can find this spiritual path and learn to follow it. We will try to understand what it is that the divine spark wishes from this life and then how to fulfill its expectations. Together with your Anamcara you will find that as you rediscover the path and start to move forward again, life will become easier and more fulfilling and you'll look back and wonder how you could ever have imagined, as you stumbled about in the undergrowth, that life was intended to be as difficult as that.

In all this work, use your intuition, listen to the Angel Whispers and discuss all this with your Anamcara. Remember that your Anamcara and many of the Celtic Angels have been with you all your life and have seen the choices you have made. Ultimately, they are your key to understanding the needs of the divine spark; they are the link between the material world and the hidden spiritual world.

When I was born

Start off your new journal by trying to paint a picture of what your family was like when you were born and as you grew up. As children we are so dependent on our siblings and parents. If you have brothers and sisters, how would you describe them when you were all children? What did they think of you and how do you think they molded you into the person you are now? You might want to talk to them about this and you'll be amazed how wrong you will be about how they felt about you.

What were your parents expecting their life to be like when you were conceived?

Your divine spark chose to be born. So we need to start there. There is no predestination about life; your divine spark did not know what would happen to it, and could only have had general expectations. So we need to understand what your parents' plans and hopes were when you were conceived.

Most of us don't talk to our parents about such things and what knowledge we have may well be more family legends than the actual truth. So there is no substitute for simply asking them. If that is not possible, you need to turn detective and talk to other members of your family, friends of your parents, coworkers or anyone else you can think of who could give you at least part of the picture.

Write down all you discover in your journal and then try to work out an answer to the question. The picture will probably not be a definite, "Well, we were going to do this, then that, then that." It is far more likely that it will be vaguer, hopes and dreams rather than schemes and plans. You may even find that they each had different ideas.

Try to find out how they thought their life would proceed. Would they move? Was it likely that they would stay together over the years? Did either of them have burning ambitions that they couldn't bear the thought of not seeing fulfilled? Those kinds of questions are quite challenging and of course memories may be faulty, but as you explore you will learn, or relearn, a lot about yourself and how you came to be the kind of person you are today.

In my case I was surprised at how easy it was to talk to my parents about this and discovered that although I was born in the very north of Scotland, both my parents, who were from central Scotland, had intended to return south. Which indeed they did when I was a boy. So my divine spark would have expected that move and it was part of my own spiritual path.

If you are an orphan or never knew your parents, then you need to assume that your divine spark expected this. You need to try to understand how you ended up with the family you did or, if you were in a children's home during your childhood, try to understand what you learned from that experience that you couldn't have learned in a more conventional family setting.

Remember, the lessons are not always pleasant. But you need to be ruthlessly honest with yourself, otherwise this whole exercise becomes worthless. You may need to go back and revisit questions that have long puzzled you. I am an only child, something I have always resented. Yet whenever I asked why my parents never had any more children, the answers I got, even as a child, never satisfied me, never seemed true. It was quite refreshing to go back to my parents as an adult, and ask them for the real answer.

What were your parents like when you were born? What traits and habits did they have?

We learn so much from our parents, even if it is only in reaction to how we perceive them to be. The person we are today is molded in no small way by the adults who surrounded us as we grew up. We therefore need to understand what it was about our parents that attracted our divine spark. My father, for example, has a restless curiosity. As I grew up he was full of ideas and schemes and would analyze every situation with the precision of the scientist he had trained to be. From him I learned to question everything and how to seek out solutions. He taught me to be a free thinker.

My mother, while an intelligent woman, preferred to spend her energies around the home and from her I learned the importance of place, especially a well-run and loving home. She was also close to her brothers and sisters and so from her I learned about extended families and the love and security they can offer.

Try to work out which of your parents' traits you have picked up and whether they are helpful or not. Even the attributes that cause us trouble now can nonetheless help us to understand how our life has turned out the way it has.

Consider where you were born and what effect that has had on you

The ancient Celts knew that the land affected you. Different land holds different magic and so your place of birth is an important factor in determining what kind of land you will feel drawn to, even if it is a reaction to your place of birth. If you were born and raised in a busy city, for example, that does not mean that you have to live in that kind of environment all your life, or that your sacred sites will all be within the city walls. It may simply mean that you will appreciate the peace, openness and tranquillity of the countryside more than someone who has always lived there.

In my case I was born in Thurso in Caithness, the most northerly town in the mainland of Scotland. There, surrounded by the soft, rolling farmland of Caithness and the bleak, open moors of Sutherland, I spent the first years of my life. When I was seven we returned south to what was, to all intents, a foreign land.

From seven to seventeen I lived near Glasgow with a strange sense that I was different from all the children around me. My birth town, Thurso, became a mystical magical place. My love of open places and the sea remained, however, and I used often to escape up onto the open moors in the hills near where I lived.

Can you remember the first friend you had?

When we are young our friends are often selected for us. They are children of our parents' friends or neighbors, or even cousins. As we grow older, however, we begin to select who we want to be friends with and while the selection may not be from a very large pool, we do nonetheless make choices.

Think back to your childhood and try to remember who you chose to be your friend and why. What was it about them that attracted you?

Can you remember people who tried to befriend you? Or people you deliberately avoided? Take time to consider each of these questions and try to understand what it tells you about yourself.

Can you remember the major decisions you took in your life?

Take a sheet of paper and, starting at the top of the page, draw a small circle. That is you when you were born. Now draw an arrow downward. What was the first major decision that you took? It may have been what school to attend or what subjects to study at that school. Of course you may have been heavily influenced by your parents or your school friends but nonetheless it was a decision that you took. So here there is a parting of the ways. Try to consider what might have happened if you had taken a different set of subjects, or attended another school. In retrospect, do you think you took the right decision? The wrong decision? Or do you think now that it wouldn't really have changed the type of person you are and how your life has proceeded? Your Anamcara might be able to help with this.

What was the next major decision? Proceed like this until you reach the present day. At every stage consider what the alternatives might have been and whether or not they would have changed your life for the better. Intuition plays a large part in this and there will be many unknowns, but still you will begin to see a pattern emerging and you may catch sight of a path flowing through your life. You might even be surprised how many different paths still end up with you as you are today!

Now look back at these decisions you have made and consider how you made them; can you detect the work of your Anamcara and Celtic Angels? Perhaps you knew you were making the wrong decision but did it anyway. Perhaps you didn't understand the implications of the decision you took but can now see that it was for the best. For example, I chose to go to Stirling University on a whim. I simply felt it was the best place for me although I was accepted by more prestigious institutions. Was that on the influence of my Celtic Angels? Probably.

What skills have I learned on my journey?

Even though we may not realize it, we learn many skills and appreciate many teachings as we proceed along our path. Some awareness may seem too insubstantial to list but do it anyway. You will be amazed at how much you have advanced.

Think of events that have happened to you and that somehow seem to stay in your mind. In my case one example is management of anger. For various reasons I am not a person who gets angry. However it did happen once. I was responsible for ensuring that a venue we were using for a show was locked up for the night and the person with the key had gone off for an hour, despite knowing we were waiting for him. I allowed myself to get more and more worked up until eventually I lashed out at the wrong person. They got angry and upset and I got angrier and more upset, but of course I was still stuck there unable to leave until the man with the key returned.

In retrospect I learned an important lesson that night and, as I say, one that I am very aware of, that getting angry doesn't solve anything. Indeed, in many ways, it makes things worse.

This, I believe, is a lesson I had to learn. It may be that I needed the calm normality to highlight this one experience. And I needed that episode in order to appreciate the teaching.

Asking your Anamcara

So far we have relied mostly on our own awareness to work on our Purpose of Life. And it may be that by now you are beginning to get some idea of how your life should be progressing. Now, however, we need to ask another. And no one knows us better than our own Anamcara.

Remember, Anamchairde are not here to teach us overtly. They do not lecture or dictate, they merely highlight and wait for us to draw our own conclusions and then to act on that new awareness.

YOUR ANAMCARA IS TELLING A STORY: A VISUALIZATION

Find a space where you feel comfortable and will not be disturbed. Light a candle and do your invocation.

For a few minutes simply be. Try to empty your mind and become aware of your surroundings. Take some time simply to relax. Now focus inward and concentrate on your breathing. Slowly breathe in through your nose.

And out through your mouth.

In.

And out.

Maintain that slow, steady, reassuring rhythm. Gradually you will realize that your awareness is drifting into a new inner peace. Welcome it and return to focusing on your breathing.

After a few more minutes become sensitive to another new awareness. Become conscious of a building. A theater. And you are entering it. The Celtic Angels whirl all around you.

The lights are dim and you are now in the small cosy auditorium. You take a seat in the middle of the row and all around you are Celtic Angels. Then there is a spotlight on the stage.

This is the story of your life, as seen and narrated by your Anamcara. The curtains open and there is a stylized backdrop. Indeed the whole production is very much in a certain style. Pause here to consider the style; it may be Victoriana, or sixties chic or puppets. There may not be actors, but cardboard cut-outs or mime artists. It may even be like a cartoon or use modern animation techniques. Appreciate the style and then let the action commence!

At the end of the production, as the curtain falls and the lights go up, you realize that once again you are back sitting in your comfortable place. Take a few moments to readjust and then, when you are ready, open your eyes. Make the sign for closure. Sit for a moment or two and then quickly write down all that you can remember from the theatre production in your Purpose of Life Journal.

Remember, the play may not be about all your life. It may just be one crucial episode. And so this is a Visualization that you may want to return to again and again as you slowly assimilate the story of your life. Remember also that there is no such thing as absolute truth. What your Anamcara is presenting is how they perceive the episode. It is only one version. Your memory will almost certainly be different. You may not even recall the event at all!

Afterward you may wish to ask other people what they remember. You may wish to discuss it more explicitly with your Anamcara. Whatever you do, and seeking independent collaboration is a good idea, ultimately you need to try to assess and appreciate the lessons you are being taught.

What would you miss if you were to become a spirit now?

We are not spirits already because there are longings we have, experiences we desire, possessions we crave. And we need to deal with them before we can progress further. Equally, it is not sufficient simply to deny yourself these delights because that does not, in the main, remove the desire, it just shows that you have strong self-restraint. No, you have to go further and come to realize that you really don't want the object of your desire.

Think of it this way: you are in a café with a friend and you see a huge dark chocolate cake on the counter. Instantly you want a piece. You hadn't thought of it before but now that you have seen it, you crave a slice. What do you do?

You choose to deny yourself a piece. You simply say, "I will not give in." And you don't. But all the way home you can barely think of the pleasure you had meeting your friend because the craving for the cake was not met.

So the following week you return with your friend to the same café. This time you have been anticipating not the fun of being with your friend, but your enjoyment of the chocolate cake. Perhaps you had no lunch so as to "earn" the cake.

To your delight they serve you an extra big helping, but even after your friend helps you out, you are still unable to eat it all. On the way home this week you feel sick, stuffed as you are with rich, gooey chocolate.

The third week your friend is a little late and you sit staring at the chocolate cake, which seems to be staring right back at you. You start to wonder why you want that cake in the first place. You're not hungry, you don't need to eat it. You come to realize that it is not the cake you want, it is the sense of pampering yourself, of having a treat. And why do you need that?

By the time your friend arrives, you have answered that question. When the waiter comes you can ask for a coffee on its own with no qualms. You no longer crave that cake.

And that is the point, of course. We can all deny ourselves pleasures, but we still want them. In order to proceed spiritually, to take a step closer to the Godhead, we need to desire the pleasure no longer. We need to be able to see through the transient, unsatisfactory nature of the enjoyment they deliver. Tragically, that is the difficult part, not the denial.

So now is the time to be honest with yourself. What would you miss most if, after this life, you were able to choose to remain a spirit?

ANAMCARA WITH SCISSORS

Find a space where you feel comfortable. Light a candle and say your invocation. Close your eyes and concentrate on your breathing. Feel yourself relax.

When you are ready, do the Angel Meditation and then go to meet your Anamcara. Explain to them that you are seeking out those things that at the moment you feel you couldn't live without. Ask for their help to aid you in letting go. Make sure that they agree before you proceed. When they are happy, present them with a huge pair of silver scissors.

Look down to your left-hand side and you will see a closed box on the ground. Inside it you know will be the first thing that you cannot let go of. Pick up the box and put it on the table. Now you realize that there is a thin, almost invisible thread that connects this to your heart. Slowly open it and take out the object. Explain to your Anamcara what the object stands for. For example, it might be a piggy bank and you realize that it stands for your love of money. More than that, you have a basic insecurity about not having enough money and so you save more and more. But you are always insecure and only now, as you think about it, do you realize that you will always fear that you don't have enough money.

Your Anamcara will discuss this with you. You will come to realize how pointless it is to hang on to this object. If you can, ask your Anamcara to cut the thread that connects that item to your heart. Your Anamcara will know if you mean it. Are you really ready?

Sometimes the answer will be no. And that is okay. This is an exercise that you need to do again and again over the years as slowly, silken thread by silken thread, you learn to let go.

Once the thread is broken the object will disappear. Place the box back on the ground and thank your Anamcara. They may want to talk some more about the symbolism of what you have just done.

However, when it is appropriate, get up and take your leave. Once you are back in your own body sit for a few minutes and then, when you are ready, open your eyes. Do your closure ceremony.

Write down all that happened in your Purpose of Life Journal.

Each time you do this exercise, it is best to have just the one box. You need to appreciate what you are doing and then

assimilate the lesson into your own life before moving on. Be patient.

What Is Your Purpose of Life?

It is not likely that the lessons we have to learn in this life are as easily expressed as "to control anger" or "to overcome greed." We are highly advanced beings already and the seven deadly sins should be no more than echoes for us. That is not to say that we don't occasionally give in and gorge ourselves on chocolate. It is just that we do not live our lives for the sole purpose of the gratification of our baser instincts.

Our Purpose of Life is likely to be far more subtle. Part of it, no doubt, is to appreciate the existence of the Godhead and the spiritual realms that are all around us. Another may be for us to begin to shift our awareness so that we try to walk in the spiritual worlds more, that we see those worlds and that we acknowledge a longing to be there. This is important because it is that longing that will eventually carry us over into the next stage of our spirit's evolution. That may not be in the next lifetime or the one after that, but it is close and getting closer.

Our Anamcara appreciates the qualities that we need to gather to ourselves and also, as we have seen, the urges and distractions that we need to let go of. However, like us, they struggle to find the words or emotions to express what this awareness is. We have to learn to be patient. You will not be presented with a list: "Do all this and you will have succeeded." Rather it is a situation that evolves and changes.

The one thing that is certain is that the more we acknowledge our Celtic Angels and work with our Anamcara, the more likely it is that we will succeed and fulfill our Purpose of Life. And, ultimately, that is what we really want.

LIVING WITH THE ANGELS

Sit with your Angel Altar and light the candles. Admire the flames. The sheer magical beauty of that ever shifting shape is bewitching. Stroke the leaves of your plant and feel the cool, calm serenity of this living creature. Dip your fingers in the earth and appreciate the power and sense of eternity there in the smallest grain. Feel the cool, languid beauty of the few drops of water as you scatter them over the plant. Light some incense and as the thin vapors slowly spiral upwards feel the shapes of the Celtic Angels as they stir around you.

You are not alone. Sense the Celtic Angels all around you. As you sit there, your Anamcara will come and sit at your side. Feel the power and resoluteness of their love for you, and know that you will succeed. Be aware, too, of the ancestors standing further behind you, eager to help and willing you to be successful. Your soul family are also out there, part of you as you are part of them.

Truly you are blessed.

As you sit there feel the emotion of the moment and give thanks. Feel your heart swell with love. And give thanks.

Enjoy that emotion.

And know you are going to succeed. How can you fail?

Afterword

Today I have finished *Anam Cara Wisdom* and it is a strange feeling. For so long the book has been part of my daily routine. I try to rise early and write until lunch. My Anamcara and I have sat and discussed the material, how to explain what we want to say and even argued over what should and should not be included. Now, today, it is all finished. And I am content.

Of course you never really finish a book like this. I have no doubt that as I continue to work with my Anamcara I will discover more about myself, my spiritual journey and the magical world around me.

When I finished *Walking the Mist: Celtic Spirituality for the 21st Century* there was a real sense of completion, of a job well done, a tale well told. This time I feel as if I have only just started. It is as if I have opened the door, stepped through and called back to you what I can see. Now I am stepping further into the space beyond.

For the Celt, it was all about the awe and magic of the worlds that surround us. On a recent trip to Ireland I discovered a sacred well at an old church dedicated to St. Benen. The church lies just outside the market town of Tuam in County Galway and I was led to it. From the old ruined church, I was drawn down to the back of the graveyard and then across a couple of fields to the old well.

I vowed I would return on my way home a few days later. And so I did, and there, on the same stone where I had sat, was a bunch of elderberries: the fruit of the angels. How strange that they should be there on the exact spot where I had sat and nowhere else.

What force, what flow makes that one event happen? How can we ever hope to understand the complex flow of life and nature that came together that day?

All we can do is marvel and accept; feel humble and thank the gods of the site. I don't truly understand the significance of the gift or how it came to pass. However, it made my day!

Now, several weeks later, I am standing on the small rounded top of the Hill o' Angels near where I live in East Lothian, looking out over the fields towards Doon Hill with the full moon bright in the autumn night sky. This huge boulder hanging in the sky, so beautiful and yet so alien, still seems so magical to me.

I look out across the land I know and understand so well and feel a deep sense of love. This is my place.

The hill has a strange magical allure that is difficult to explain. There is a sweet melancholy about this place. A sadness that is comforting; a sense of peace that nourishes you.

Here my Anamcara and I are content. We feel connected to the land underneath us, the Celtic Angels who skirl around us and the spiritual realms who seem so close here on this small hill.

Working with the Celtic Angels has been an incredible and beautiful time for me that I have been happy to share with you. And so I take the book and I offer it up. I offer it to the gods and goddesses of this site. To the Celtic Angels who come to this special place. I offer it to the memory of those most amazing of men and women who lived as Druids and monks and nuns tending the sacred sites of the Celtic lands here and throughout Western Europe. But most of all, dear reader, I offer *Anam Cara Wisdom* to you. Cherish it, love it. But, above all else, enjoy!

The Celtic Circle

Why not join the Celtic Circle Yahoo! group? This is a mailing group where all the latest news about Donald McKinney's talks and workshops are posted. Other information includes advance notice of days for special celebrations, such as new moons, full moons, Celtic fire festival days and any other excuse for a party. Also posted are any other items of news or events that might be of interest.

Find out more at www.celtic-circle.com or http://groups.yahoo.com/group/thecelticcircle.

Further Reading

The Druids warned against the dangers of writing down any-thing important. In our modern world, however, so much knowledge and personal experience has been committed to paper. Here are some of the books that have informed, inspired or simply made me question my own preconceptions. But simply because it is written down does not make it true. Only you can decide on that.

CELTIC, GENERAL

Carmichael, Alexander, *Carmina Gadelica*, five volumes, Oliver and Boyd, Edinburgh, 1928.

ANGELS, GENERAL

Briggs, Constance Victoria, *The Encyclopedia of Angels*, Plume, New York, 1997.

Collins, Andrew, *From the Ashes of Angels*, Bear & Company, Rochester, VT, 2001.

Cooper, Diana, *Angel Inspiration*, Hodder & Stoughton, London, 2001.

Guiley, Rosemary Ellen, *Encyclopedia of Angels*, Facts on File, Inc., New York, 1996.

Virtue, Doreen, *Healing with the Angels*, Hay House, Carlsbad, CA, 1999.

CELTIC SAINTS, ANGELS AND ANAMCARA

Matthews, John, *Drinking from the Sacred Well*, Harper San Francisco, New York, 1998.

Nagy, Joseph Falaky, *Conversing with Angels and Ancients*, Cornell University Press, Ithaca, NY, 1997.

Sellner, Edward C., *The Celtic Soul Friend*, Ave Maria Press, Indiana, 2002.

Other Books from Ulysses Press

The 7 Healing Chakras: Unlocking Your Body's Energy Centers

Brenda Davies, M.D., $14.95

The 7 Healing Chakras explores the essence of chakras—vortices of energy that connect the physical body with the spiritual.

Be Your Own Psychic: Tapping the Innate Power Within

Sherron Mayes, $13.95

Offers lessons on understanding and programming dreams, acting on hunches, gaining true insight, and following a deeper guidance.

Portable Reiki: Easy Self-Treatments for Home, Work and on the Go

Tanmaya Honervogt, $14.95

Presents do-it-yourself, step-by-step treatments for quick, effective Reiki healing—anytime, anyplace. The book's system is specially designed to help busy people release stress, improve health and restore personal energy.

Psychic Shield: The Personal Handbook of Psychic Protection

Caitlín Matthews, $14.95

Provides simple and commonsense strategies for overcoming negative thinking, dealing with difficult people, becoming attuned to spiritual guidance, and protecting one's inner peace.

To order these books call 800-377-2542 or 510-601-8301, fax 510-601-8307, e-mail ulysses@ulyssespress.com, or write to Ulysses Press, P.O. Box 3440, Berkeley, CA 94703. All retail orders are shipped free of charge. California residents must include sales tax. Allow two to three weeks for delivery.

About the Author

DONALD MCKINNEY is the author of *Walking the Mist: Celtic Spirituality for the 21st Century*. He is the convener of the Celtic Circle, one of the largest global Celtic networks and is a former lecturer in Spanish history and politics. Since 1986 he has actively pursued a spiritual path. His experiences, which saw him transformed from an atheist, have totally changed his life. He now works with earth energies, spirits and trees and sees them as major tools in helping spiritual awareness and development to occur. He lives with his partner in Scotland and is a partner in Body & Soul, Scotland's foremost New Age business. He gives talks and workshops all over the United Kingdom, Ireland and North America.

Share your Celtic Angel experiences! Donald McKinney would love to hear from you. If you have any questions or just want to tell your stories, please get in touch. You can contact him via his website: www.donaldmckinney.com.